PHARMACEUTICAL SALES MANAGEMENT IN A CHANGEABLE MARKET PLACE

Vincent F. Peters
Thomas B. Yeats

BLACK DOG
Publishing Company
Downingtown, Pennsylvania

PHARMACEUTICAL SALES MANAGEMENT IN A CHANGEABLE MARKET PLACE

Vincent F. Peters
Thomas B. Yeats

Credits

Editor: Vincent F. Peters
Layout and Composition: Joseph C. Peters
Cover Design & Artwork: Cody® ,Fairfield, NJ

© Copyright 2000, by Peters, Vincent F and Yeats, Thomas B

Printed in the United States of America

Peters, Vincent F., and Yeats, Thomas B

Pharmaceutical Sales Management In A Changeable Market Place

ISBN 0-9656231-2-2

Pharmaceutical Sales Management *'in a changeable marketplace'*
Contents

Pharmaceutical Sales Management *'in a changeable marketplace'*
Contents

Pharmaceutical Sales Management *'in a changeable marketplace'*
Contents

CHAPTER 1 REPRESENTATIVE TO MANAGER

I. OVERVIEW OF THE PHARMACEUTICAL INDUSTRY

These are challenging times for the pharmaceutical industry. New products, increased pressure from competition and generic substitution, stringent government controls, and the concept of managed care have combined to make the task of selling pharmaceuticals in the 2000's a difficult one. Today's ever-changing global marketplace demands more highly trained sales professionals than ever before. Training will not only prepare sales professionals to meet these challenges, but will also have a very strong impact on sales and profits.

Recently there has been a paradigm shift: where previously there was relative stability in the pharmaceutical industry, change is now the norm. Takeovers and mergers are commonplace. Historically, the pharmaceutical industry has been a product-focused industry; however, more emphasis is now being placed on disease states, treatment programs, and customer services. An environment of cost effectiveness and therapeutic advantage has replaced the previous issues of efficacy and safety. The trend in hospitals is toward converting inpatients to outpatients of home-health recipients and emphasizing prevention rather than corrective medical treatment. District Sales Managers are the vital link for ensuring that, via the road of training and development, the pharmaceutical sales representative becomes more that just a technical expert but that they emerge as a problem-solver for the physician. More than ever before, sales representatives must earn the confidence of the customer through relationship building. Selling selectively and delivering a well-reasoned, compelling message which are keys to success.

District Sales Managers are responsible for making sure that this knowledge and training in these skills are provided and utilized.

Today's ever-changing global market demands more highly trained sales professionals than ever before.

More emphasis is now being placed on disease states, treatment programs, and customer services.

It is crucial the District Sales Manager is constantly striving to improve his/her knowledge, skills and habits.

It is crucial that the District Sales Manager is constantly striving to improve his/her knowledge, skills and habits, while also developing a positive mental attitude towards self improvement.

The major aim of this learning system, is to provide guidelines for the District Sales Manager to follow, so that they develop the necessary experience, to competently and confidently deal with a rapidly growing and changing marketplace.

Objectives

The following objectives are provided to identify expected learning outcomes. When you finish this section you should be able to:

Successful District Sales Managers must make the adjustment for training and developing new and experienced salespeople themselves.

1. Describe the major responsibilities of a District Sales Manager.
2. Describe the four basic management functions.
3. Describe the difference between being a successful Sales Representative and a successful District Sales Manager.

Key Concepts

1. Successful District Sales Managers must make the adjustment for training and developing new and experienced salespeople themselves.
2. District Sales Managers are part of a sales and marketing management team and support senior management's decisions.
3. District Sales Managers appraise and evaluate sales performance.

District Sales Managers motivate the sales force to achieve planned sales objectives.

4. District Sales Managers motivate the sales force to achieve planned sales objectives.

A. Position Description–Managing vs. Operating
The Change from Rep to Manager

The challenges of being a district manager in a pharmaceutical company are never ending, it is by far, one of the most involved jobs in the industry. You are managing people which is very difficult, each person has their own personality and ideas, all people are different. You have to adapt quickly to the fact that you are no longer a sales rep, you are now a manager. To better understand what this means, we need to first define, what is management?

Managing evolves around four basic management functions/activities: planning, organizing, leading and controlling. These are the four basic functions of managers, no matter what industry they are in. <u>Management has often been defined as "getting things done through others."</u> This is the biggest change that you have to be convinced of, you are no longer a Sales Representative selling. Your job is to manage a team of sellers. If is difficult, because many times super sales people are made District Sales Managers, and this involves a change in mind set.

The job of District Sales Manager means that you are responsible for a geographic area or district. Your sales representatives need to make calls on doctors, hospitals, HMO's, etc, in this district, and obtain sales objectives for you. This area is far too large for one person to cover, so you have a team of sales reps to do the job.

It is your job to plan, organize, lead and control your sales representatives, so that they can do the best job possible. Their success in achieving results, reflects on your perceived image as a manager. As the old saying goes, "show me a sales rep, and I will show you his or her's manager." What the saying really means, is that sales reps are only a good as their District Sales Managers. In the job of the District Sales Manager, it is your responsibility to do everything in your power to help your representatives be as successful as possible. This handbook was specifically designed to help you make the transition from sales rep to manger, and to be as successful as possible.

Managing evolves around four basic management functions/activities: planning, organizing, leading and controlling.

It is your job to plan, organize, lead and control your sales representatives, so that they can do the best job possible.

B. Resilience of the District Sales Manager

We will cover all of the areas that we believe crucial to successful managing. This learning system covers a wide range of topics, demonstrating the resilience required of a District Sales Manager.

I.   Representative to Manager
II.   The Home Office
III.   Planning and Organizing
IV.   Territory & Time Management
V.   Recruiting and Hiring
VI.   Communications
VII.   Leadership & Motivation
VIII. Controlling
IX.   Performance Appraisal
X.   Training New Representatives
XI.   Conducting Effective Sales Meetings

The concept of the pharmaceutical District Sales Manager has changed greatly over the years.

To better understand the job of a pharmaceutical District Sales Manager, let's look at the job and its responsibilities.

The concept of the pharmaceutical District Sales Manager has changed greatly over the years. The job was first looked at as someone who was responsible for the sales in units and prescriptions, and worked in the field with reps to ensure that they made successful sales calls. The prime objective was to get the sale, which did not make the job much different to that of a sales rep. The responsibilities have since then changed dramatically. The District Sales Manger's job requires an individual with not only great people skills, but also, a lot more business savvy than just monitoring the sales activities of their sales reps. The District Sales Manager needs to also have a vision, business planning and financial skills, to enable them to handle their district as a profit center. The District Sales Manager needs to be in tune with the needs of the marketplace. The district manager needs to have relationships not only with sales reps, and management, but also with colleagues, and more and more so with physicians and customers. The District Sales Manager's job involves many relationships.

The District Sales Manager needs to also have a vision, business planning and financial skills to enable them to handle their district as a profit center.

The job of the District Sales Manager involves many different roles and responsibilities. The manager is involved in planning the work for the district, assigning tasks to sales reps, evaluating the sales rep's work, the upholding company policies, setting the district budget as well as having the responsibility for achieving sales results.

The challenge of becoming a District Sales Manager is exciting. There is a lot of prestige that goes along with the job, and with this prestige is status, authority, more money, and increased visibility in the organization. There is also a lot of pride involved in the job. The satisfaction of seeing your people advance and get promoted because of your good coaching and managing. There is a great satisfaction of leading the team to achieve

results. The job provides you with an enhanced feeling of success. The job of District Sales Manager also provides you with the opportunity for greater professional and personal growth. It opens up doors for you to interact with other levels and disciplines of management in the company.

Today's District Sales Manager has more of a role of an executive as well as an operations manager. We need to avoid doing everything ourselves, and rely on the sales reps to carry out these functions. For example, if we are about to launch a new product, many activities are involved. Besides establishing territorial sales and unit sales objectives, there has to be a plan for who does what, and when. We can only reach the sales and units forecasts for products, if we have adequate personnel. The term for the utilization of this personnel is called organizing and then delegating. The dictionary definition of delegation is to send or appoint as a deputy or representative to assign or entrust an act or be carried out.

If we are to launch the product successfully, there are many leadership criteria that need to be met, such as communicating, co-ordinating and training.

The manager is involved in planning the work for the district, assigning tasks to sales reps, evaluating the sales rep's work, as well as having the responsibility for achieving results.

Besides establishing territorial sales and unit sales objectives, there has to be a plan for who does what and when.

The District Sales Manager is constantly using the four basic management function activities of:-
* **Planning**
* **Organizing**
* **Leading**
* **Controlling**

During the entire launch sales cycle, we must have <u>controls</u> in place. Controls to measure how we are doing. Are reps meeting their quota? e.g. what do we need to do better? If the objectives are not being met, what corrective actions do we need to take? So during this whole launch sales cycle, the District Sales Manager is constantly using the four basic management function activities of:

* Planning
* Organizing
* Leading
* Controlling

We need to go back and evaluate these activities. If our sales show we are not achieving our objectives, we may have to modify our plan, and organize the sales group differently. When another new cycle comes along, we start the process of planning, organizing, leading and controlling, all over again.

As we said in the beginning of this chapter, these four basic management/function activities are imperative no matter what type of management job we are in. To be successful as a District Sales Manager, we also need to be completely aware of the job responsibilities. A job description is critical, and we will spend some time looking at the job of District Sales Manager. We urge all managers to have a job description that completely explains what they are supposed to do. Experience has shown us that people fail for two reasons: first, they do not know what they are supposed to do, and secondly, they do not know how well they are doing. Make sure that you have an accurate and up to date job description. If you feel that it is not accurate, tell your supervisor, and sit down with him or her and rewrite it, most companies will have no problem with this.

To be successful as a District Sales Manager, we also need to be completely aware of the job responsibilities.

An example is provided in the text that follows.

II. Managing or Operating (Checklist)

Quite often, managers new and experienced have difficulty in deciding between the elements of managing and non-management functions in their daily work activities. The additional pressures in today's work environment, of doing more with less people and other resources can force managers to participate in non-managerial functions. Complete the following checklist and select the items that you consider to be managing functions as opposed to non-managerial, or operating functions.

	Managing	**Operating**
1. Calling on an account with one of your sales rep's to show the customer that company management is interested in the account.	❑	❑
2. Making a product presentation to a doctor in order to show a sales rep how to do it.	❑	❑
3. Making an individual call on the chief pharmacist of a large hospital to build customer relationships and promote business.	❑	❑
4. Explaining how to solve a work problem that one of your sales rep's has just brought to you.	❑	❑
5. Filling out a form to recommend a salary increase for one of your sales rep's.	❑	❑
6. Explaining to one of your rep's why he or she is receiving a salary increase.	❑	❑

Managers new and experienced have difficulty in deciding between the elements of managing and non-management functions in their daily work activities.

Select the items that you consider to be managing functions as opposed to non-managerial, or operating functions.

	Managing	Operating
7. Interviewing a sales candidate referred to you by an employment agency.	☐	☐
8. Giving a telephone progress report to your sales manager.	☐	☐
9. Asking one of your sales rep's what he or she thinks about a selling idea that you have.	☐	☐
10. Planning and deciding on a dollar sales objective by account.	☐	☐
11. Deciding what the cost budget request shall be for your sales team.	☐	☐
12. Reviewing monthly reports to determine progress towards specific sales objectives.	☐	☐
13. Deciding whether to meet a competitive price based on considerations beyond what the salesperson has access to.	☐	☐
14. Deciding whether to recommend adding a position.	☐	☐
15. Designing an improved sales office layout.	☐	☐
16. Asking your sales people to establish tentative six month objectives for the number of personal sales calls made on target accounts.	☐	☐
17. Giving a talk at a local college on career opportunities in the pharmaceutical industry.	☐	☐

District Sales Managers can only be successful if they recognize that their role is that of a trainer, not of a salesperson and adapt accordingly.

	Managing	Operating
18. Transferring an account from sales rep X to sales rep Y because sales rep X did not devote the necessary effort to develop the account.	☐	☐
19. Phoning an HMO to request help in solving a customer delivery problem for one of your sales rep's.	☐	☐
20. Planning the extent to which your sales rep's should use staff services during the next year to accomplish overall sales objectives.	☐	☐

District Sales Managers must train others to sell not seek opportunities to show off their own skills as a Salesperson. This is one of the common failings among new District Sales Managers.

Managing or Operating

Managing by getting results through others can take place through:-

Motivation

Delegation

Training

Counseling

Communicating

Suggested Answers

Now let's take a look at the suggested answers (with explanations) to the managing versus operating activities.

1. **Operating.** This may be a highly necessary activity, but it is selling not managing. The direct purpose of the call is not to get results through others.

2. **Managing.** This is training.

3. **Operating.** This is selling. The direct purpose is not to get results through others.

4. **Managing.** This is supervising, assuming the manager does not have his/her people come to him/her, so that he or she can feel sufficiently productive for routine solutions or recurring problems which they are capable of handling. It would be counselling if a more formal, planned personal discussion were needed.

5. **Operating.** The actual filling out of the form is clerical. Instructing your secretary how to fill it out would be a managing activity in that it would be delegating.

6. **Managing.** This is motivating.

7. **Operating.** This may be an essential activity, but the manager is actually performing a personnel function in the same way that he or she is selling when he calls on accounts. When he of she interviews, he or she is not currently getting results through others. Deciding to hire someone after all the recruiting and selecting has been done, however, would be considered a managing activity.

8. **Managing.** This is communicating for the purpose of control, provided the manager is doing so to receive possible guidance an direction. Otherwise it may be plain communicating, which everyone does, manager or not.

9. **Managing.** This is communicating, probably in order to develop a selling program, and it could be a form of motivating if the manager's main purpose is to have the sales rep participate in developing the idea in order to get later acceptance.

10. **Operating.** The manager is developing objectives which is a managing activity but he or she is not delegating; he or she is developing objectives by account which his/her sales reps should be best qualified to do since they work closely with the accounts. Were he or she to review the sales objectives of one of the sales reps, he or she would be managing, in that he would undoubtedly be planning in part of an overall sales objective to beaccomplished by the sales reps as a group.

11. **Managing.** This is planning-developing a budget. Putting the budget in its proper form would be clerical.

12. **Managing.** This is measuring and evaluating.

13. **Managing.** This is probably coordinating-making sure that any price deviations are consistent with an overall plan. However, this would be an operating activity if procedures and controls could be set up in such a way that certain pricing decisions could be delegated.

14. **Managing.** This is developing the organization structure.

15. **Operating.** This is a methods engineering function. Deciding to get an improved office layout would be a managing activity.

16. **Managing.** This is developing objectives as well as standards of performance.

17. **Operating.** This is performing a public relations function.

18. **Managing.** This is correcting-taking corrective control action. This could also be considered the disciplining part of supervising.

19. **Operating.** This may not be necessary, but it is the inside part of a sales rep's job. The direct purpose of the phone call is not to get results *through*, but rather for your sales rep.

20. **Managing.** This is developing a program of marketing strategy to achieve group results.

As you can see, the difference between managing and operating can be subtle in many instances. Indeed, two District Sales Managers can appear to be performing identical activities, yet, we would say 'that one is managing and the other is not' - depending on whether or not the intent is to get results through others, or for others.

As you can see, the difference between managing and operating can be subtle in many instances.

Yet, we would say 'that one is managing and the other is not' - depending on whether or not one's intent is to get results through others.

III. District Manager's Job Description

Introduction

The District Sales Manager is expected to successfully perform in his/her position, completely filling all requirements, carrying out all managerial functions, implementing the procedures and policies of upper management.

The District Sales Manager is expected to successfully perform in his/her position, completely filling all requirements, carrying out all managerial functions and generally implementing the procedures and policies of upper management. However, before the manager can perform efficiently, he or she must be advised of the many specific responsibilities of his/her position. The manager's awareness should be followed by his/her complete understanding and commitment to his/her responsibilities and duties. Only then can the District Sales Manager be prepared to carry out the varied duties of his/her position.

In order to provide the District Sales Manager with a complete understanding of his/her duties, the following Job Description has been prepared. The description includes specific information on the manager's organization relationships, his/her broad functions, and his/her specific responsibilities including those to be implemented in the field.

The job description should be reviewed and discussed.

It is recommended that the Job Description be provided to the District Sales Manager for his/her corporate personal view. At the appropriate time and meeting place, the job description should be reviewed and discussed by the manager and upper management. Such a meeting should eliminate any misunderstandings and answer any questions that the manager may have concerning his/her management position. The ultimate results of the interchanges should be increased efficiency and complete commitment by the District Sales Manager.

The ultimate results of the interchanges should be increased efficiency and complete commitment by the District Sales Manager.

A. Organizational Relationships

1. Reports directly to the Regional Sales Manager, business unit director, sales manager, or another assigned member of management.
2. Directly manages the activities of the field sales staff assigned to him/her.

B. Broad Functions

1. To assure the achievement of all company goals and objectives within his/her area of responsibility.
2. To effectively manage the sales staff for which he or she is responsible, ensuring each person's growth and development to the fullest extent possible.
3. To select, train and maintain a sales staff fully capable of achieving corporate objectives.
4. To assure the proper introduction and promotion of all company products and the necessary follow-up through promotional activities.
5. To promote through the sales staff and his/her own personal efforts, the company image to the physician, the pharmacists, and paramedical personnel, primarily, and consumer secondarily.

To select, train and maintain a sales staff fully capable of achieving corporate objectives.

C. Specific Responsibilities

1. To recruit, hire and train (under the direction of the Regional Sales Manager) pharmaceutical sales representatives in order to maintain an effective sales team in his/her district.
2. To be certain that each member of his/her sales staff is working his/her territory in the most efficient way possible. This means that the District Sales Manager determines whether or not each pharmaceutical sales representative is fully meeting all of his/her territorial responsibilities (fully explained in the pharmaceutical sale's representative's position description).
3. To keep his/her sales staff fully informed, at all times, of all company policies and procedures and to be certain that they are being followed to the fullest extend.
4. To establish sales goals and objectives for each person (under the direction of the Regional Sales Manager) on a monthly, semi-annual, and annual basis and to work closely with him/her to successfully accomplish each.
5. To keep the sales staff fully informed on the results of their sales efforts on a continuing basis, being certain each person clearly understands whether he or she is or not achieving his/her specific sales goals and objectives.

Specific Responsibilities

To recruit, hire and train

To establish sales goals and objectives for each person on a monthly, semi-annual, and annual basis and to work closely with him/her to successfully accomplish each.

C. Specific Responsibilities (cont)

Specific Responsibilities

To develop and co-ordinate.

To review and appraise each person

To hold sales meetings.

To utilize performance appraisal data.

6. To develop and coordinate (under his/her supervisor's guidance) an effective plan of action for each sales cycle. Then, to inform his/her sales staff of each new sales plan (if not accomplished by his/her superior) and work closely with each person in achieving the desired sales promotional goals.

7. To review and appraise each person's sales performance on a semi-annual basis (under the direction of his/her supervisor). To conduct discussions with each person on his/her sales activities for this period in a friendly and informal atmosphere. To compliment each person on the areas of good performance, help him/her identify areas in need of improvement, and develop a plan of action for the person to achieve the desired goals and objectives.

8. To work on the organization and reorganization of each sales territory whenever it is necessary to do so to better achieve corporate objectives.

9. To train each member of his/her sales staff in product knowledge, selling skills, territory planning, and all the essential areas of territory management.

10. To hold sales meetings (when directed by the Regional Sales Manager) designed to present the current promotional sales plan, to discuss important corporate matters, to determine the effectiveness of the plan of action already in progress, etc.

11. To utilize performance appraisal data in making salary and special bonus or commission recommendations with management.

12. To recommend termination of representatives who violate company policy and those who, after a reasonable period, are unable to meet important sales performance standards-subject to consultation with manager.

13. To assume other responsibilities that are specifically assigned to him/her by his/her immediate supervisor.

D.   Field Sales Operational Responsibilities

1. To check reports and sales results of each person on a continuous basis, so as to ensure adherence to overall plans and objectives. To promptly investigate deviations and take corrective action.

2. To work with each pharmaceutical sales representative soon after the receipt of sales bulletins, plan, etc and attendance at sales meetings, to be certain the plans and programs are understood and are receiving the full support of each person.

3. To plan and maintain an efficient schedule for field sales and administrative activity.

4. To participate in the overall planning and scheduling of field sales training and sales meeting programs.

5. To submit, as necessary, complete plans for sales territory changes and sales personnel requirements, indicating an effective plan of action for each.

6. To consistently analyze the sales results by products, trade class, and sales territory and the factors influencing the results. As necessary, to make recommendations to management for revisions or sales strategy changes in order to accelerate sales progress.

7. To keep sales management well informed on all phases of field sales activity, such as the individual progress of each person, competition, attitudes of the medical profession, etc. by means of scheduled field trip progress reports.

8. To develop a position of trust and confidence with each member of the field sales staff. To encourage a free exchange of ideas, listen attentively to problems, and offer guidance in helping each person solve specific field sales problems.

9. To strive to keep aware of the unique traits and personality characteristics of each pharmaceutical sales representative and to give due consideration to these factors in supervising each person's sales activities.

10. To develop and maintain friendly relationships with influential personnel of key accounts, hospitals, and clinics in each sales territory.

Field Sales Operational Responsibilities

To plan and maintain an efficient schedule for field sales and administrative activity.

To consistently analyze the sales results by products, trade class, and sales territory and the factors influencing the results.

To develop a position of trust and confidence with each member of the field sales staff.

Once you have taken over a new district, you may wish to do an complete evaluation of the district to check the status quo. You are now aware of your responsibilities through your job description, and conversation with your management, so you are now ready to conduct an evaluation of your district.

You are now aware of your responsibilities through your job description and conversation with your management.

E. The District Management Evaluation

The District Management Evaluation is nothing more than an inventory of activities required of a sales organization and an analysis of the skills, knowledge and attitudes needed by sales management, (refer to Chapter 3, pages 47-48).

Rationale

Whenever a sales objective is not met, invariably problems with the sales operation exist. There are always problems – sometimes serious – with 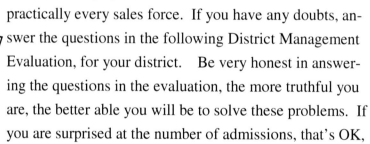 practically every sales force. If you have any doubts, answer the questions in the following District Management Evaluation, for your district. Be very honest in answering the questions in the evaluation, the more truthful you are, the better able you will be to solve these problems. If you are surprised at the number of admissions, that's OK, at least you are on the way to effective sales management – because you are being proactive by analyzing problems and opportunities. Use the space marked "Comments" for planning future activities. No doubt there are criteria of your own that you would like to include in this evaluation.

This exercise will help you to analyze your own strengths and pinpoint areas where you can improve or develop additional managerial skills.

Answer the questions on the following pages as truthfully and objectively as you can. You will be the only one to see the answers. This exercise will help you to analyze your own strengths and pinpoint areas where you can improve or develop additional managerial skills.

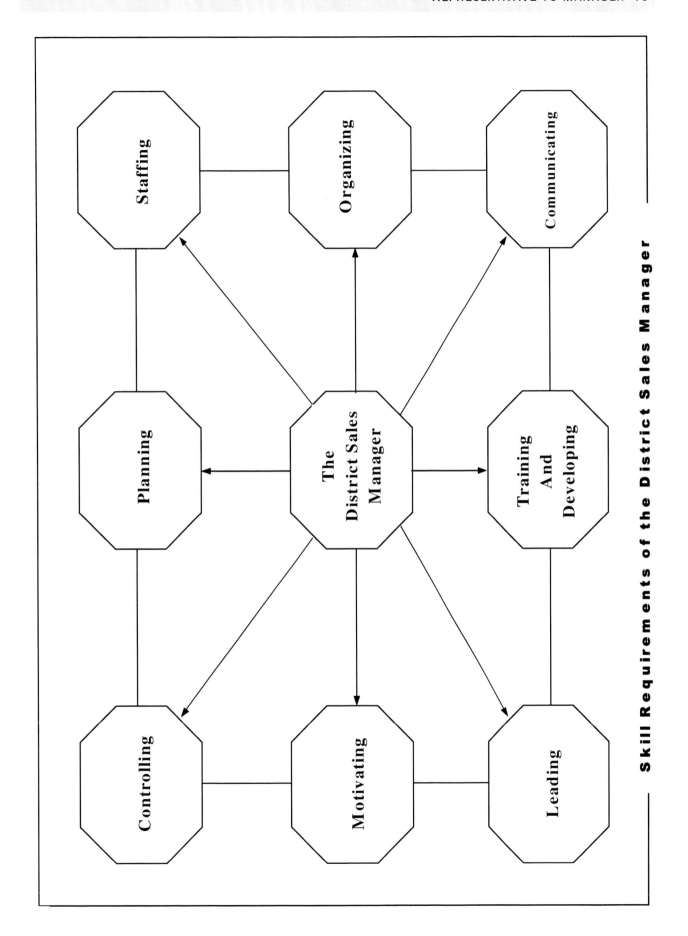

Skill Requirements of the District Sales Manager

The District Sales Manager's Customers

INTERNAL	EXTERNAL
Higher Management	Doctors
Financial Dept	Patients
Marketing Dept	Pharmacy
Medical Dept	Customers
Distribution Dept	Hospitals
Legal Dept	Health Care Professionals
Registration Dept	Distribution Channels
Production Dept	Drug Committees
Purchasing Dept	Trade Organizations
Packaging Dept	Advertising Agencies
Administration	Government Departments
	Sales Team
	Customs

Summary

The District Sales Manager holds a crucial position and the job involves many different roles and responsibilities. It requires an individual with not only exceptional interpersonal skills but also a lot of business know how.

The District Sales Manager is involved in planning the work for the district, assigning specific tasks for Sales Representatives and evaluating each Sales Representatives performance. Successful managers understand and accept that the needs of the company are best met when the needs of the individuals that they manage are met. District Sales Managers need to have a vision, business planning and financial skills to enable them to handle their district as a profit center.

Successful District Sales Management in a nutshell is all about 'getting profitable results through others'.

Review Questions (Chapter I)

DIRECTIONS. Circle the letter corresponding to the correct answer for each question.

1. An environment of cost effectiveness and therapeutic advantage has replaced the previous issues of efficacy and safety.
   a. True
   b. False

2. Less emphasis is now being placed on disease states treatment programs and customer service.
   a. True
   b. False

3. Which of the following is not a District Managers responsibility?
   a. To appraise and evaluate sales performance
   b. To motivate the sales force to achieve planned sales objectives
   c. To train and develop experienced sales representatives
   d. To strive to constantly improve their knowledge or skills

4. Managing evolves around four basic functions.
   a. Organizing, planning, following, controlling
   b. Planning, organizing, leading, controlling
   c. Controlling, planning accepting, organizing
   d. Organizing, marketing, controlling, planning

5. The definition of management is:-
   a. Exceeding your sales budget each year
   b. Training sales representatives to develop into managers
   c. Getting profitable results through others
   d. Taking on the role of an executive

Answers to Review Questions

1. A

2. B

3. C

4. B

5. C

II. THE HOME OFFICE

I. INTRODUCTION

We have many tools available to us to help make our jobs more productive and effective. One very important tool is the home office. Consider the home office to be your base of operations, and like any other organization that has people in the field, a base of operations is very important. You are in charge of field operations for your district, and you need a place where you can direct these operations, a place away from the formal office environment.

> Consider the home office to be your base of operations.

Today, the home office is becoming more and more popular than ever before, in fact many people have taken up what is known as "telecommuting". Telecommuting is working out of a home office, and communicating and conducting business activities via, phone, fax and e-mail. Telecommuting very seldom involves people ever going to the head office, except for special meetings etc. In this chapter we will look at the District Sales Manager's home office, and see exactly what you need, and also provide you with ways to set up the office. The home office is a very effective tool, and can be considered to be your lifeline for communications and administrative activities, between the field and the head office.

> Telecommuting is working out of a home office, and communicating and conducting business activities via, phone, fax and e-mail.

Objectives

The following objectives are provided to identify expected learning outcomes. When you finish this section you should be able to:-
1.   Describe the term 'telecommuting'.
2.   State the rule for handling all mail.
3.   Describe the list of items suggested for the file cabinet.

Key Concepts

1.   The home office provides a base of operations for creating best practice.
2.   The home office allows the manager to contribute to the development of a workplace learning environment.

The increased amount of administrative duties and paperwork, demand that the manager do more and more administrative type work each day. Since we recommend that you spend 70 to 80% of your time in the field with your sales reps, this boils down to about one full day a week for administrative duties. Many companies allow District Sales Managers to use Fridays as a "desk day". A day where you will spend your entire day handling administrative procedures, so you will need a formal office set-up, if you are to work effectively. The home office will also be used at other times during the week, for evening phone calls, e-mails, faxes, and to handle follow-up matters. Your job as District Sales Manager puts you square in the middle of the actions between the field force and the home office. In fact, you are constantly in communication with a very large and diverse group of people. You are required to deal with different departments in the head office on a variety of issues. In addition to communicating and dealing with your sales management, you will on occasion have to be in contact with other departments, such as: marketing, human resources, training and marketing services.

Your job as District Sales Manager puts you square in the middle of the actions between the field force and the home office.

You may be required to deal with outside agencies that are handling special promotional programs for the company. On occasions you will have to deal with job candidates who are seeking employment in the company.

You are constantly in communication with a very large and diverse group of people.

Your daily administrative activities involve handling of mail and messages, some of which requires an immediate response, and others that can wait. Examples of daily mail that would involve an immediate response are: customer inquiries, rep expense account reports, sales management and head office requests. There is also plenty of standard information mail that you need to read, but do not need to take action on, read it and either file it or discard it. These days there is also an ever increasing amount of junk mail that arrives every day, scan it, because you never know, it may contain information on a new book on pharmaceutical district management. Go through you junk mail quickly, and discard it, otherwise it will pile up and become a time waster.

A good general rule to follow with all mail, is to only handle each piece of mail once. Look at it, write comments on it, and forward it or discard it. Follow-up with sales rep requests immediately.

We have talked a lot about mail here, but you really do not need a home office to receive mail. What you do need in an effective home office set-up are the following: a telephone (preferably with a phone/fax line dedicated just to your business activities), an answering machine, a computer with fax and e-mail capability, a desk, a desk lamp, a clock, a file cabinet (with loads of file folders), ample amounts of paper, pens, post-it notes, paper clips, and other stationery supplies. Another very important item that I like, is a large bulletin board of the entire district, with territories outlined, highlighted and numbered, and plenty of colored map pins to mark the position of special customers and clients. The last item that you need is a metal storage shelf. The marvels of e-mail have really increased our communication capabilities, but they have also caused us to over communicate. We find ourselves frequently communicating on matters that in the past we would have postponed if we had to write a note or a fax. Handle all e-mail and phone messages on an as needed basis, prioritize them and respond to them according to their importance.

A. Your Workday in the Home Office

Your workday in the home office needs to be very well planned and organized, if you are to be effective. We refer to this specifically in the chapter on Time Management, that you need to develop a "To Do List" well the "To Do List" applies here. Plan your day and set objectives, and prioritize those objectives. Items considered to be of high priority are: assignments that have specific due dates, requests from head office personnel, requests from customers and sales management, and of course, requests from your sales reps. Routine paperwork from sales reps that should always be moved along quickly are items such as orders, expense reports, requests for additional promotional materials or samples. On occasion you will have to send out weekly district bulletins urgently, so make this a top priority.

A good general rule to follow with all mail, is to only handle each piece of mail once.

The marvels of e-mail have really increased our communication capabilities, but they have also caused us to over communicate.

We refer to this specifically in the chapter on Time Management, that you need to develop a "To Do List".

Plan your day and set objectives, and prioritize those objectives.

Two items that should be done on a regular basis, and with ample time allocated are: planning of fieldwork, and district meetings.

There are items that should be done every day on a regular basis, such as the review of sales figures.

You need a good file drawer first of all in your desk, for items that you need in a hurry, such as territory sales reports, special requests and follow-up actions.

The next item of critical importance, is the file cabinet. Ideally with four large drawers where you will be able to file away a variety of items.

Each drawer should be set up in the following way, with the items of most importance and most used, in the top drawers.

Items such as rep weekly reports, candidate resumes, clinical papers etc, can all be read and reviewed after you have handled the high priority items mentioned above. Two items that while they do not need to be reviewed urgently, should be done so on a regular basis, and with ample time allocated are: planning of fieldwork, and district meetings.

Obviously there are items that should be done every day on a regular basis, such as the review of sales figures. The list goes on and on, and if you look at it, it is incredible how many administrative items you handle on a regular basis. Items such as rep vacation schedules, sample accountability, performance appraisals, field coaching forms, doctor dinner meetings and symposia, training sessions and other special projects. To handle all of these items effectively, you need a couple of good filing areas for document storage. You need a good file drawer first of all in your desk, for items that you need in a hurry, such as: territory sales reports, special requests and follow-up actions, the current cycle plan of action, routing information, and or any sales rep problem or disciplinary action that requires immediate attention. These items need to be at your finger tips and readily available at a moment's notice.

Make sure that you have a large file drawer in your desk with folders that you can store all of these important items, have the files labeled for your convenience and easy identification.

B. The File Cabinet

The next item of critical importance, that we mentioned earlier is the file cabinet. You need to have a large file cabinet in your office, ideally with four large drawers where you will be able to file away a variety of items. We will attempt to provide you here with the suggested organization of the file cabinet and its contents. Starting from the top drawer down, each drawer should be set up in the following way, with the items of most importance and most used, in the top drawers. The first drawer for example should contain items that you need to get your hands on relatively quickly, such as: your expense budget, special promotion programs, your hospital and HMO accounts, special client and customer information, such as VIP doctors and opinion leaders. Other items that can be in this first drawer are current (most recent) expense account forms, POA forms, district meeting notes and ideas, training information, and business correspondence. Each of these items should have its own file folder in the drawer.

The second drawer should be set up in the following fashion and include primarily information on all of your reps and their territories. You will want to have a file folder for each territory and along with it, a file folder for each rep in that territory. In the territory folder, you will have a small map of the territory, and other information such as sales figures, major account info etc. The rep's file folder should include information on their performance and salary guidelines. The rep's folder should also be used for field coaching, and contain the latest field coaching form.

The next drawer should be dedicated primarily to product information. In this drawer you should have folders for each of your products. In these product folders there should be promotional brochures, and memos, as well as clinical reprints relevant to the product. You also may wish to have another folder with information on competitive products, including brochures and reprints that the competition is currently using.

The last drawer is a good place to keep items such as sales reports by territory, for the year and other forms that may be required. Have a folder for each territory where you keep the sales reports, and another for expense reports. You may wish to use the back section of the drawer for blank forms such as: field coaching forms, employment applications, sample and materials request forms, blank expense account forms, etc.

C. The Metal Storage Shelf

In addition to the file cabinet and desk, I like to see every

District Sales Manager have a metal shelf to store items. These metal shelves are economical and can be purchased anywhere. They are very handy for storing extra supplies and stocks company literature. Each manager should have an ample supply of promotional literature and reprints on hand, in case one of his/her reps need some in an emergency.

The second drawer should be set up in the following fashion and include primarily information on all of your reps and their territories.

The rep's file folder should include information on their performance and salary guidelines.

The next drawer should be dedicated primarily to product information. In this drawer you should have folders for each of your products.

The last drawer is a good place to keep items such as sales reports by territory, for the year and other forms that may be required.

Each manager should have an ample supply of promotional literature and reprints on hand, in case one of his/her reps need some in an emergency.

In fact it would not be a bad idea that each manager have the same shipment of promotional materials that a rep receives each cycle. The shelf can be located in the manager's office, or if not possible or practical in their basement or garage. These shelves also keep promotional materials clean and safe from damage. You may wish to have a locked storage cabinet in place of the metal storage shelf, if you want to store product samples. This cabinet should be locked at all times, especially if you have small children in the house.

I hope that we have been able to emphasize the importance of the home office, and that we have provided you with ample guidance in how to set up a home office.

The home office provides a lifeline for administrative activities and essential communications and allows for 'frontline management' in a sane environment.

Summary

A very important tool to help the District Sales Manager manage more effectively is a well set up home office which allows the very busy manager to telecommute; the modern approach to maximizing communications and conducting business activities via phone, fax and e-mail.

The home office provides a lifeline for administrative activities and essential communications between the field and the head office and allows for 'frontline management' in a sane environment.

Review Questions (Chapter II)

1. Telecommuting's primary purpose is to help the district manager to:
   a. Spend less time driving
   b. Reduce frequency of trips to the home office
   c. Spend more time on paperwork, and less time in the field
   d. Conduct business activities with the home office and field without necessary travelling

2. The ideal recommended percent of time that should be devoted to administrative duties weekly, is
   a. 30 percent
   b. 20 percent
   c. 50 percent
   d. 10 percent

3. If you are storing samples in your office, they should be in a locked cabinet.
   a. True
   b. False

4. Each representative's file folder should contain the following:
   a. A map of their territory
   b. Sales figures and major account info
   c. Field coaching forms
   d. All of the above

5. The District Manager should have a supply of the current cycle's promotional materials and literature.
   a. True
   b. False

Answers to Review Questions

1. B

2. B

3. A

4. D

5. A

III. PLANNING AND ORGANIZING

I.   Management Planning Process

Management planning is a continuous on-going process, that involves many elements: forecasting, setting objectives, action planning, modifying the plan, implementing, controlling, corrective actions, and achievement of objectives. We are going to look at each of these elements, and examine them in detail.

Planning Module

*   Sales forecasting
*   Setting objectives
*   Action planning
*   Controlling
*   Implementation of the plan

We all agree that the pharmaceutical marketplace is becoming more competitive and busy every day. Now with the flurry of new high tech products that the industry is bringing out, we have more challenges than ever, which makes good planning even a higher priority. We and our sales reps need to have plans, long and short term plans. As the old saying goes, "plan your work and work your plan."

Objectives

These learning objectives will help you focus your attention on learning outcomes. After completing this section you should be able to:
1.   Describe the factors that can affect district sales.
2.   Describe the criteria for setting objectives.
3.   Name six elements that are involved with the planning process.

Key Concepts

1.   The District Sales Manager is responsible for planning objectives and action plans for the team.
2.   The most important task of a District Sales Manager is Planning.

Management planning is a continuous on-going process, that involves many elements:

forecasting,

setting objectives,

action planning,

modifying the plan,

implementing,

controlling,

corrective actions

and achievement of objectives.

A. Sales Forecasting

We are of the opinion, the best forecasts come up from the field.

District managers are required to do some type of sales forecasting for their districts, but the extent or degree of forecasting will vary from company to company. Very often, the forecast is sent down from management and the sales force has had very little involvement in its development. We are of the opinion, the best forecasts come up from the field, and not the other way around, basically, because forecasting from the field is more realistic.

No matter what forecasting method your company uses, the methodology requires certain activities and thought processes to ensure its accuracy. One of the most critical situations that can occur, is that if we erroneously forecast sales either too high, or too low, this leads to unrealistic objectives being set, in turn causing a negative impact on the sales force.

When you start forecasting you need to write down all information that could have an effect on the sales in your district.

When you start forecasting, you need to write down all information that could have an effect on the sales in your district. You need to look at all of the factors that can affect the sales in the district.

1. The Political Situation

Has anything happened in your district, that could have a negative or positive effect on sales?

Has anything happened in your district, that could have a negative or positive effect on sales? For example, cutbacks or increases in government funded programs.

2. The Economic Situation

How will your sales be impacted by these measures.

How is the economic and employment situation in your district, are corporate downsizing measures, a factor? How will your sales be impacted by these measures.

B. The Pharmaceutical Marketplace

You should try to list all factors that could have an impact on the market segments in which your products compete. What growth trends and marketing opportunities exist? Populations change, America is a very mobile society. New large homes can suggest children, another market opportunity for pediatric products, and products for women of child bearing age.

List all factors that could have an impact on the market segments in which your products compete.

1. The Competition

The competition becomes more aggressive everyday, but there is enough business out there for everyone. Keep an eye out for what methods other companies are using to promote their products. What new products are scheduled to be launched, and what impact will they have on our business in the district? We need to keep an eye on sales force size too, virtually all companies are expanding their sales forces, how will this effect us?

Keep an eye out for what methods other companies are using to promote their products.

2. The Company's Sales and Profits

How well the company is doing, has a great impact on our sales forecasting, we need to have sufficient information on past sales and trends, if we are to see the future clearly.

There is a need to look at the products individually and their position in the product life cycle. New products tend to experience rapid growth, old more established products will grow at a slower steady pace. Do we have products that have plateaued? Are our older products under attack from newer high tech products, or at least products that are perceived as more high tech, because they are newer? In order for you to forecast as accurately as possible, you need to be aware of the marketing departments marketing plans and strategies for your products, as well as any new promotional activities that are to be introduced.

There is a need to look at the products individually and their position in the product life cycle.

You need to be aware of marketing's plans and strategies for your products.

After you have reviewed all of these elements and factors, you are ready for the next very important activity, setting objectives.

C. Setting Objectives

All objectives need to be quantitative and qualitative

Setting objectives is the most important element in the planning process, and it determines depth and intensity of our sales activities. We like to use the SMART criteria in setting objectives. Keep in mind that we need objectives that are long and short term, if we are to build the business. All objectives need to be quantitative and qualitative, if they are to be effective. Let's take a look at the criteria:

1. Specific

Objectives should be clear and understandable to all, and have specific completion dates.

The objectives should be clear and understandable to all, and have specific completion dates. Let's look at an example, many people put down that they will increase sales in their district or territory, but this is really not a well stated objective. A better stated objective would be to increase sales of product X, by 10% in units, over the same time period last year.

2. Measurable

Objectives need to be measurable.

Objectives need to be measurable, and we should even make qualitative objectives as measurable as possible. In the example above, the quantitative objective is measurable. Quite often we see qualitative objectives that we will increase our reps product knowledge, this objective can also be made more quantitative if we word it as follows: ensure that each rep achieves a minimum score of 90% on the product X exam. Keep in mind, that many qualitative objectives depend on the district managers observation, and can be subjective at times.

3. Achievable

Objectives have to be achievable.

Objectives have to be achievable, if they are not, we run the danger that we will de-motivate the sales force. Setting sales targets too high can be demotivating.

4. Realistic

Objectives need to be realistic, and this goes along nicely, with achievable. It is not realistic to expect large increases in sales of an older product that may not have any new clinical supporting data.

Objectives need to be realistic.

5. Timely

All objectives need to have a time frame, if they are to be considered well written. For example: achieve a 15% increase in the sales of product Y, by the end of the second quarter of the year.

All objectives need to have a time frame.

The last thing that we need to keep in mind with all objectives is that they need to support management's objectives. We need to follow the plan of action very closely and ensure that we are in synch with management's objectives. Once we have set our objectives, we are ready to move on to the next step, which is action planning, the action plan tells us how we are going to get where we want to go.

D. Action Planning

1.   The action plan tells us the following:

* Who will do What
* How will it be done
* What Resources are required
* Where and when will it be done

We need to follow the plan of action and ensure that we are in synch with management's objectives.

You as the district manager, play the most critical role in motivating, helping, and training sales reps in their jobs. You help them to plan their work, and to implement the plans and achieve their objectives. Besides helping the sales reps develop their plans, the district manager needs to plan his/her work extensively.

2.   There is an ongoing need to plan field work to determine:

* How much time do you need to spend in the field?
* How much time do you need to allocate to each rep?
* How often do you conduct field visits and for what period of time?
* What are the objectives of each field visit?

There is a real need to plan field work.

3.   There is also a need to plan performance appraisals for each rep covering:

*   Date, place, and time?

*   How do you initiate the conversation?

*   How do you proceed with the evaluation?

*   What issues or points of disagreement do you anticipate?

*   How do you respond to these issues?

Plan performance appraisals for each rep

Once the planning is complete and the implementation takes place, we need to ensure that the proper controls are in place.

E. Controlling

Control is not really effective, unless the proper actions are taking place and the desired objectives achieved. This careful monitoring through control can lead to the following situations:

*   First, the objectives are being achieved, and things can move on ahead.

*   Second, the objectives are not being met, and the following alternative actions need to take place:

     - Actions must be corrected in order to accomplish the desired objectives, the plan is not being implemented properly.

     - The original action plan needs to be modified, it was not realistic and will not help achieve the objectives.

     - The original objectives have to be modified because they are unrealistic and unachievable.

Control is not really effective, unless the proper actions are taking place and the desired objectives achieved.

What usually takes place, is that the objectives are usually achieved in their original or modified form. If the original objectives were found to be unrealistic or unachievable, a whole new round of objective setting takes place, and the cycle continues.

F. Considerations for the Implementation

There are four considerations involved in the successful implementation of the plan with the sales force:

* The organization of the sales force
* The manpower availability
* Implementation through sales force administration
* Territory coverage

1. The Organization of the Sales Force

You generally inherit a sales force that has already been organized in a specific fashion. You may reorganize or reshape the existing organization to improve productivity. You usually are not involved in completely organizing the sales force, unless it is a new start-up situation.

 No matter what the situation, there are some good principles of sales force organization, that you should adhere to, and they are as follows:

* Every territory should be profitable. It should return a profit after all expenses have been paid. A territory should never be subsidized by other territories, with the only exception to this principle being a new territory that may be going through some temporary difficulties.

* Each territory should suit the personality of the sales representative who works it. Reps need to feel satisfied, motivated and challenged in their territories. Each territory needs to attract and hold the attention of each person who works it.

* Every territory has to be clearly defined with specific boundaries, and not overlap surrounding territories. When there is an overlap, we have problems among reps, and even more importantly with doctors and other customers. Each territory by the same token should be protected, (reps should get credit for all business in their territory, unless otherwise specified).

There are four considerations involved in the successful implementation of the plan with the sales force:

The organization of the sales force

The manpower availability

Implementation through sales

Territory coverage

Every territory should be profitable.

Every territory has to be clearly defined with specific boundaries.

Territories should be as equitable as possible.

* Territories should be as equitable as possible, their sales potential should be roughly equal, and the logistics of working them should also be equal. One territory should not be easier to achieve high sales results and another barely able achieve quota, with the same amount of sales effort. When territories are not equitable there is friction and conflicts in districts.

* Territories need to be manageable. A territory should not be so large, that high potential accounts can not be satisfactorily covered during the promotion cycle. This situation leads to a territory's potential not being fully exploited.

* Every territory should have an infrastructure of adequate transportation in place, from the reps home to high potential doctors and other customers.

Territories need to be manageable.

2. TERRITORY DATA AND INFORMATION

If we are going to set up territories in this manner, we need to have available to us the necessary territory data and information. This data and information should include:

* Population concentrations
* Economic conditions and purchasing power by area
* Cities, suburbs, and towns with the highest potential
* Locations of the doctors, pharmacies, hospitals, managed care facilities, and wholesalers with the highest prescribing and /or purchasing potential
* Transportation and communication facilities
* Socioeconomic growth and health care development, and their expected impact on the future sales potential in different areas.

Each territory should have an infrastructure of adequate transportation in place.

G. How Do We Assign Reps To Territories

There are certain criteria that we need to take into account when assigning reps to territories, they are as follows:

1. Experience and talent: The most experienced and talented sales reps should be designated the most important and difficult territories. These assignments should be readily accepted by reps, and considered a challenge worthy of their superior experience.

    These top reps should also have a say in choosing the territories that they prefer to work in, as realistically as is possible.

2. Personality: There are certain personality traits that make it preferable for a sales rep to work in one type of geographical area, over another. Reps should have the following characteristics in different types of territories, for example:

An Urban Territory
*   Is a team player
*   Likes cities
*   Is cosmopolitan
*   Is sophisticated
*   Doesn't mind not seeing the direct results of his/her efforts

A Rural Territory
*   Likes to work alone
*   Is a self-starter
*   Is able to make decisions independently
*   Likes rural areas
*   Likes to see direct results of his/her efforts
*   Characteristics of the doctors and accounts in the territory: People in some areas don't like outsiders, a sales representative who is from the area will be better accepted. There are also instances when customers are more open to people who are not from the area, and in fact may even be more influenced by someone else.

> The most experienced and talented sales reps should be designated the most important and difficult territories.

> Personality: There are certain personality traits that make it preferable for a sales rep to work in one type of geographical area, over another.

Sometimes it is better to not relocate sales representatives, if it is an area where their families are happy.

* Roots: sometimes it is better to not relocate sales representatives, but to keep them where they have their roots and origins, especially if it is an area where their families are happy.

At other times, there are circumstances that do not always seem fair, for example:

- When you do not assign a representative to an area that they want and deserve, but to a more difficult territory, because you need their talent and expertise.

- Or also by asking a representative to move or relocate to a far away territory, against their will, because the territory requires someone with their particular qualities.

If you do have to move sales reps to geographic areas that are not of their choice, they should understand why it is necessary, and be convinced to readily accept the assignment.

If you do have to move sales reps to geographic areas that are not of their choice, they should understand why it is necessary, and be convinced to readily accept the assignment.

The question is frequently asked, how often should sales reps be rotated? We all know that it takes a certain amount of time for a representative to become productive in a territory. Many experts believe that it takes about six months to a year on the average. Then it takes another year and a half to reach maximum productivity in the territory. This is usually so, because:

- It takes time for reps to get around the territory rapidly
- Reps need to develop good relationships with doctors and accounts
- Reps need to develop good time schedules and itineraries

For a representative to become productive in a territory. Many experts believe that it takes about six months to a year.

Everyone will agree that reps should not be moved from a territory, as long as they are productive, because this will avoid a drop in sales and also add the unnecessary cost of relocation. The moving costs are only part of the problem, the other part is that new reps are less productive in a new territory, although this is only a temporary situation.

Many people believe that if reps are in a territory for too long of a time period, they become bored and unproductive. It is believed that they become too friendly with their doctors, and start to rely too heavily on relationship selling.

A word of caution here when we talk about moving sales reps around. On the one hand we are telling reps to do long range planning, and then on the other hand we are talking about moving them. Doctors and other customers like to deal with sales reps on a long term basis, in fact, they really do not like it when companies are always moving reps around. It is very hard to build long term relationships, and the trust and confidence that go along with this, so think twice before you move reps around. One of the best things that you can do to avoid reps getting bored, and unproductive, is to give them new responsibilities. It can be as simple as having them help you with the training of new reps in the district. Or by having them help you conduct a district meeting.

You also may wish to look at the manpower distribution of your reps differently.   For example, does it make more sense to have reps who are generalists, or product or key account specialists? There are no yes or no answers to this question, but nevertheless, it is an issue that district managers face everyday.

H. Implementation of the Plan

We have seen how we need to organize territories and assign people to them. Now we need to look at the implementation of the sales and marketing plan to achieve company objectives.

Proper implementation of the sales and marketing plan requires that we do the following:

- Ensure that all members of the sales force understand and support all action plans

- Ensure that they have the materials and tools, visual aids, samples, and in sufficient quantity.

- Coordinate all activities at levels within the sales force

- Supervise the execution of all action plans

- Follow up all requests from doctors and accounts in the field

A word of caution here when we talk about moving sales reps around.

Doctors and other customers like to deal with sales reps on a long term basis, they really do not like it when companies are always moving reps around.

To avoid reps getting bored give them new responsibilities.

There are no yes or no answers to this question, but nevertheless, it is an issue that district managers face everyday.

Ensure that all members of the sales force understand and support all action plans.

So for us to be successful in implementing all of these actions, we need to do a range of things, such as:

- Proper implementation of the cycle plan

- Proper selection and classification of doctors

- Prospecting for new doctors and accounts

- Routing and adequate territory coverage

- Good record keeping

- Accurate call reporting

Crucial in all these activities, are the critical success factors of good leadership, motivation, communication and training, because without them, you can not be successful.

Crucial in all of these activities, are the critical success factors of good leadership, motivation, communication and training, because without them, you can not be successful.

I.   Effective Territory Coverage

We can never cover a territory too well. Due to the nature of the beast, territories are very dynamic entities that are constantly in a state of change. Effective territory coverage can be defined as the particular actions that are required in the sales reps area of responsibility when carrying out the marketing and sales plan.

Included in these actions are: travel, call planning and preparation, doctor calls, pharmacy and wholesale calls, service calls, follow-up calls, and the updating of doctor and account record cards.

The only way to execute these activities effectively, is through optimization of routes and itineraries.

All of these tasks need to be done within the normal framework of the overall company plans, but they also need to be planned in much more detail, in order to take local territorial conditions into account. The only way to execute these activities effectively, is through optimization of **routes** and **itineraries**. So what do we mean , when we say routes and itineraries? A **route** can be defined as a sequence of places visited within the territory, and connected by the specific roads and highways used to get there. An **itinerary** is the series of times and dates when these places are visited.

There are many advantages to using good routes and itineraries, for example:

- - There is better coverage of high potential doctors and customers
- - Travel times and expenses are reduced
- - Reps have a better chance of achieving their objectives
- - There is more time available for effective promoting and selling
- - The sales to expenses ratio is improved
- - Reps lose less time in between calls
- - Control is improved, because district managers know where their reps are

J. The Routing Procedure

Routing is one of the most effective ways that sales reps can work in our competitive environment, it has been used successfully by sales reps from other industries for many years. The pharmaceutical industry has also embraced the routing procedure and found it to be another way to increase sales force productivity.

There are some procedures involved when setting up your routes that can make your life a lot easier. First of all you need to have a good map that covers the reps entire territory, this map should be very accurate and show cities, towns, major roads and all streets. Make sure that the map is as up to date as is possible. Many reps like to put the map in a clear plastic transparent cover or sheet protector, so that you can write on it with a marker, and erase it easily without damaging the map. You next want to mark on the map in color, the areas where your high potential doctors and customers are in the territory. Pick different colors to indicate where your medium potential doctor and customers are located. Follow this technique for all other customers of importance whom you visit on a regular basis. You next need to study all the roads that connect these customers, to find the most effective way to cover them all. The objective of this procedure is to reduce unnecessary travel time, and to ensure that we are visiting the high potential doctors and customers as often as necessary.

There are many advantages to using good routes and itineraries.

Routing is one of the most effective ways that sales reps can work in our competitive environment.

You need a good map that covers the reps entire territory

Mark on the map in color, the areas where your high potential doctors and customers are in the territory.

Find the most effective way to cover them all. The objective of this procedure is to reduce unnecessary travel time as much as possible.

Its your job to ensure that your reps know how to use routing as effectively as possible.

There is a lot of flexibility in the use of this procedure and its your job to ensure that your reps know how to use routing as effectively as possible. It is the responsibility of the district manager to ensure that the most effective planning is being used in his/her district. You have to involve your reps in this planning process to ensure understanding and get their buy in.

Routes need to be reviewed on a regular basis and be updated according to changes in the territory.

Routes need to be reviewed on a regular basis and be updated according to changes in the Territory. Frequently, the changes are due to changes in the population, doctors, pharmacies, other important customers move to another area. Areas also experience economic growth and decline due to these changes in the population. So when you revisit targeting and doctor selection with your reps, you can also help them to make the routing changes too. You may find that while the routes change, it also may necessitate a change in the territorial boundaries too.

It is not uncommon for the reps to not want to change the structure of their territories or routes, nobody likes change. The better you understand why reps resist this change, the more effective you will be in helping them.

The better you understand why reps resist change, the more effective you will be in helping them.

Typically, reps resist for the following reasons:

* Restructuring routes and territories is hard work
* Working an *established* route is convenient
* Sales reps don't like to lose contacts that they have developed over the years
* Sales reps frequently fear that new boundaries and routes will increase their workload, and hurt their sales

It is your job as district manager to convince your reps that by making these changes, they will be more effective and more productive and thus earn more.

It is your job as district manager to convince your reps that by making these changes, they will be more effective and more productive, and thus earn more.

K. Itineraries

We said earlier that itineraries consist of the dates and times that different doctors and customers along routes should be visited. There is an obvious interrelationship between routes and itineraries. The best routes for visiting certain areas has an impact on the dates and times when they are visited. By the same token, a route could be determined by the fact that key doctors and clients can only be visited on certain days or times.

When you establish itineraries within routes, you need to consider the following:

* The total time that it takes to see doctors and accounts in each place along the route
* The need to avoid certain holidays
* The days and times when leading physicians and customers are generally available
* The appointments that can be made

Reps need to be trained to be punctual and manage their time efficiently when they work routes and itineraries. Working routes and itineraries effectively will help them maximize company sales and profits, and increase their earnings.

You need to consider the following:

* **The total time that it takes to see doctors and accounts in each place along the route**

Reps need to be trained to be punctual and manage their time efficiently.

Summary

The six P's

Proper

Planning

Prevents

Particularly

Poor

Performance

The pharmaceutical marketplace is an ever evolving process and so is the planning process. This process involves the various elements of forecasting, setting objectives, action planning, modifying plans, implementing and controlling, taking corrective actions when necessary and appropriately, and the achievement of company, district and territory objectives.

Planning takes the form of short term and long term and because of the volatile market place we live in, constant adjustments and refinements need to be implemented for the good of all concerned, this is not always obvious but it is always necessary.

The most important task that all District Sales Managers have is planning; without utilizing the six P's, a District Sales Managers will never achieve their full potential. Whilst planning is the most important task, a District Sales Manager must ensure that he/she has the necessary skills in organizing, directing, leading, training and developing, making decisions and controlling the district operations.

District Managers Evaluation Checklist

A. Are you and your sales reps developing plans based on sufficient data?

Yes ☐   No ☐   Comments

B. Do you have an ongoing program for obtaining qualitative data
(e.g physician attitudes, needs)?

Yes ☐   No ☐   Comments

C. Are there well formulated objectives for your entire operation?

Yes ☐   No ☐   Comments

D. In turn, does every sales representative have clear and well – formulated
objectives?

Yes ☐   No ☐   Comments

E. Does each sales rep have an updated physician classification list?

Yes ☐   No ☐   Comments

F. Does each sales rep know whom to contact and when?

Yes ☐   No ☐   Comments

G. Are there standards of performance for each sales representative and
yourself?

Yes ☐   No ☐   Comments

H. Is there a plan for key accounts (e.g. major hospitals, HMO's)?

Yes ☐   No ☐   Comments

I. Do you ensure that all sales reps are planning their own time to the best
advantage?

Yes ☐   No ☐   Comments

J. Do you adequately plan your own time and have a well–developed
system of priorities?

Yes ☐   No ☐   Comments

K. Do you plan (and conduct) meetings so as to ensure optimal use of time and effort?

Yes ☐   No ☐   Comments

L. Are there any other planning responsibilities you deem very important? Please list and evaluate the present condition of this responsibility.

Yes ☐   No ☐   Comments

Review Questions (Chapter III)

DIRECTIONS. Circle the letter corresponding to the correct answer for each question.

1. Management planning is a continuous ongoing process that involves:-
    a. Meeting at the end of each year to review the company's performance.
    b. Deciding the amount of incentive to be paid at the end of the year.
    c. Many elements including sales forecasting, setting objectives, action planning, controlling and implementing the plan.
    d. Having a quarterly budget meeting.

2. Factors that could have an effect on the sales in your District.
    a. The political situation
    b. The economic situation
    c. Competitive activity
    d. All of the above

3. Action planning tells us the following:-
    a. Who will do what
    b. How will it be done
    c. What resources are required
    d. All of the above

4. The acronym for setting objectives is:-
    a. Specific, maintainable, achievable, realistic, time framed
    b. Specific, measurable, achievable, realistic, timely
    c. Specific, measurable, acceptance, relevant, timely
    d. Specific, maintainable acceptable realistic, timely

5. The Six P's stand for:-
    a. Perfect practice prevents particularly poor presentation
    b. Proper practice prevents particularly poor performance
    c. Proper planning prevents particularly poor performance
    d. Perfect planning prevents particularly poor presentation

Answers to Review Questions

1.   C

2.   D

3.   D

4.   B

5.   C

IV. TERRITORY AND TIME MANAGEMENT

I. THE PHARMACEUTICAL MARKETPLACE

Marketing refers to the way companies design, package, promote, and distribute their goods. The pharmaceutical industry develops and manufactures products for treatment and promotion of human healthcare and may be marketed to medical professionals, institutions, or consumers themselves. A particular product may be targeted to more than one market; and people may be treated or take medications for one or more indications.

Marketing refers to the way companies design, package, promote, and distribute their goods.

Objectives

The following objectives are provided to identify expected learning outcomes. When you finish this section you should be able to:

1. Describe the factors that affect the marketplace.
2. Name the four phases of a product cycle.
3. Identify the main, sources for obtaining data on the pharmaceutical marketplace.
4. Specify how Walsh International provides physician – based information.
5. Describe the electronic sales management system call PRECISE™.

A. Factors that Affect the Marketplace

It is the responsibility of the marketing department to continually research and analyze the company's business environment and to provide other departments, including the sales force, with relevant and timely data needed to be competitive in the marketplace. Each company must be fully informed of the nature of the

---
KEY POINT
Factors that affect the marketplace include socioeconomic factors, technological developments, the legal and regulatory environment, nature of the marketplace, products, patent life, buying system, and competition.

Marketing department collects, disseminates data to be competitive.

market, the company's position within the market, and the position of its various products, as well as past, present, and forecasted trends. A product manager is generally responsible for gathering and using this information.

Many factors influence the marketplace

Some of the important factors which influence the marketplace are listed below.

Socioeconomic factors. This category includes demographic factors such as the average age of the population, the general educational level of the population, changing social attitudes, fads, income levels, and other characteristics of people's lives. Additional people-related issues are the preferences of the buyers and the users, the indications for purchase and frequency, motivation needs and desires, perceived risks and rewards, influence of authority figures, product image, and others.

Socioeconomic – changing demographics and preferences

Technological – new discoveries, developments

Technological developments. New technologies can influence fads and preferences and can render a previous product obsolete almost overnight. This is particularly true in some industries such as computers, telecommunications, and biotechnology.

Legal and regulatory environment. As mentioned previously, bringing a new drug to the marketplace is costly and time consuming. There are many restrictions on products used to treat human medical conditions. Federal regulations govern the development, labeling and marketing of all pharmaceuticals.

Legal – federal and professional regulations

Marketplace dynamics – buyers, prices, profits, advertising

Nature of the marketplace. The market itself includes issues such as who buys and uses the product, size and structure of the market, how a product is priced, what kind of profit can be earned in that market, effective distribution channels, regional and seasonal differences, effects of advertising, and many other issues.

Products. The product may be targeted towards a unique market and it may have many competitors. Some products come in many varieties and may be substituted with generic drugs or with similar products.

Products – competitors and substitutes

Patent life. Typically, the proprietary or patent ownership on a new drug will extend for about 20 years, during which time competitors may not duplicate the product. This is necessary in order for the manufacturer to earn substantial profits to recover at least some of the expenses involved in development of the drug. When the patent expires, the original manufacturer may turn over the formula or the technology for generic production and will no longer earn significant revenue from the drug.

Buying system. Individual consumers generally have a pattern of buying which involves a conscious or subconscious decision-making process. This begins with identifying a perceived need and ends with the selection of one or more products to meet that need. A company may target the buyer in one or more steps in that process to promote its products. Institutional or professional buyers have a buying system that is usually more structured, or even set by policy or law. A sales representative will need to know what that system is for each buyer.

Competition. Knowledge of the products, services, strengths, weaknesses, and activities of competitors is vital for determining marketing strategy, especially in the area of OTC pharmaceuticals where prices are generally determined by a competitive, market-driven economic structure. The marketing department must know how to set prices appropriately.

All of these factors contribute to the overall life of a pharmaceutical product. Most products have a life cycle of four recognizable phases: introduction, growth, maturity, and decline. For example, Product A is a new peptic ulcer therapy that is an anti-microbial that kills *H*. pylori, a bacterium associated with ulcer disease. When introduced, Product A was the only

> **KEY POINT**
> There are four phases in the life of a product: introduction, growth, maturity, and decline.

anti-microbial on the market. After its introduction, sales soared as the recognition of a treatment for peptic ulcer therapy became widespread. Over time, the sales leveled off-the product 'matured'. Within 2 years, there were 4.

**Patent life –
revenues earned
during first 20
years.**

**Buying system –
customer's
purchasing pattern
and procedure**

**Competition – market-driven
economic structure**

**Phases of product
life: introduction
growth, maturity,
decline.**

Two major sources of marketing data: IMS, Walsh

B. Sources of Marketing Data

Sales managers and the marketing department rely on pharmaceutical marketing data that is supplied from external sources. Two of the major international companies that provide marketing information for the industry are IMS (International Medical Statistics) and Walsh International.

These two companies provide specific statistical information on product movement, prescription direction, and physician and hospital – based information. They provide this information to assist the industry in marketing and monitoring its goods and services.

IMS produces 3 reports

1. **International Medical Statistics (IMS).** IMS generates several different reports: the American Pharmaceutical Industry Report (API), American Medical Index (AMI), and PROFITS reports. All of these reports provide useful information for the pharmaceutical industry.

American Pharmaceutical Industry report. The API report gives the company a comprehensive and reliable survey of healthcare products, both prescription and nonprescription, supplied to healthcare outlets. Data in each of the following areas are reported:

API report provides monthly survey of prescription and OTC products

* leading manufacturers

* leading products

* new products

* drug by manufacturer

* therapeutic class summary

* share of therapeutic class

* product index

* sales volume and dollar values by pack in therapeutic categories

> **KEY POINT**
> **IMS provides the API, AMI, and PROFITS reports. The API report provides a survey of both prescription and OTC drugs supplied to healthcare outlets. The AMI report provides marketing information such as trends in prescription patterns, changes in brand or generic preference, and other aspects of the marketplace. The PROFITS report provides a way for managers to measure the performance of a sales representative.**

The report is produced monthly and provides the latest information by month, year-to-date (YTD) and moving annual total (MAT) for the total national pharmaceutical industry.

American Medical Index report. The AMI report provides the marketing department with information that allows the product manager to accurately define markets, to determine the most effective produce positioning for existing of new products. The medical index provides trends in prescribing patterns, changes of brand or generic preference, dosage details by indication, and both physician and patient characteristics. This report allows marketing and product managers to respond to changes in the marketplace, plan selling strategies, evaluate promotional activity, target the audience accurately, and monitor the competitors' strategies and activities. Sales management also benefits from AMI through the enhancement of their ability to evaluate regional differences in physician behavior and disease occurrence, profile target physicians, and optimize sales activity.

AMI report provides trends in prescriptions, preferences, indications

Marketing managers use data to plan strategies.

PROFITS report. PROFITS is a management tool with applications for both sales and marketing; it provides extensive, reliable data which is easy to read. It is the only system that accurately measures the performance of a sales representative. The flexibility of PROFITS enables changes to territory boundaries and provides the sales department with the data they need for a prompt response to any significant market changes.

KEY POINT
The PROFIT report derives its acronym from:
Pharmaceutical
Representative
Oriented
Flexible
Index of Territory Sales

PROFITS measures sales performance by territory

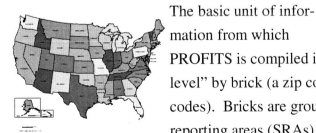

The basic unit of information from which PROFITS is compiled is "dollar sales at peak level" by brick (a zip code or grouping of zip codes). Bricks are grouped together to form sales reporting areas (SRAs), which are then combined to create a representative territory or expand a state or national total.

Through SCRIPTRAC, Walsh Int'l provides physician-based prescribing data

2. Walsh International. Walsh International is the world's largest supplier of physician-based information. Through its SCRIPTRAC services, Walsh provides pharmaceutical companies with the opportunity to segment the physician audience and optimize promotion efforts. This targeting provides information on prescribing habits, innovation by the physician (new protocols, etc), attitudes and patient demographics. SCRIPTRAC helps a pharmaceutical company identify and promote to the target audience that uniquely matches its strategic product plan at less cost than collecting the data itself.

> **KEY POINT**
> **Walsh International uses SCRIPTRAC to track physician-based information such as prescribing habits and patient demographics.**

The pharmaceutical marketplace is changing

As we enter the 21st century, the pharmaceutical industry is facing substantial pressure, and the nature of the market which it has so effectively served in the past is changing due to escalating research and development (R & D) costs, shorter effective product life cycles, regulatory convergence, and evolution of a healthcare buyers market.

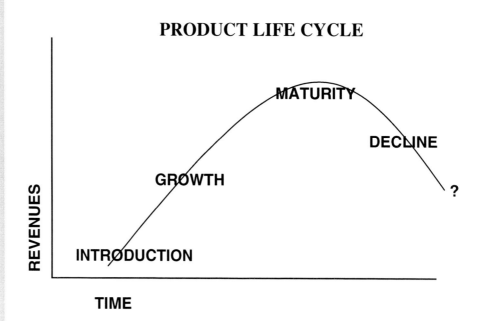

The physician is at the center of this complex process which delivers prescription medicine to the patient. The changing environment means that there is a need to know more about each doctor, the influences and restrictions on that doctor, and the practice demographics. It is no longer satisfactory to promote to physicians as a homogeneous group. To maximize the effects of the promotion, it must be tailored to the individual physician's needs. This is true micromarketing.

Selling must be targeted to individual physician's needs

3. PRECISE™. PRECISE is a popular sales management system used throughout the world. Companies select it because PRECISE has the most comprehensive range of territory and sales force management facilities available. PRECISE provides an electronic territory management system for the representatives, including appointment schedules, call history, physician records, and other features. PRECISE also offers a sales force management system for the managers by providing reports and analyses. PRECISE is an international industry standard.

> **KEY POINT**
> **PRECISE provides an electronic territory management system for representatives, including appointment schedules, call history, and physician records.**

PRECISE is an electronic territory management system

Summary

It is important for District Sales Managers to understand about marketing – the ways that companies design, package, promote and distribute their goods. The District Sales Manager is charged with ensuring that the sales team implement the marketing plan as directed. It is also important for the sales team to use the statistical information that is provided via IMS and Walsh, to help them sell more effectively and selectively.

Review Questions

DIRECTIONS. Circle the letter corresponding to the correct answer for each question.

1. Factors that affect the pharmaceutical marketplace include all of the following, **except**:-
   a. Business goals of executives
   b. Changes in social attitudes
   c. Competitive products after the patent expires
   d. Government regulations

2. The life of a product has four phases: introduction, growth, maturity, and:-
   a. Decline
   b. Expiration
   c. Profit Stability
   d. Revision

3. There are several important sources of pharmaceutical marketing data. A comprehensive monthly report on prescription and non-prescription healthcare products is the:-
   a. America Medical Index
   b. American Pharmaceutical Industry
   c. International Medical Statistics
   d. PROFITS

4. Walsh International provides SCRIPTRAC services, which track the:-
   a. Attitudes and prescribing habits of individual physicians
   b. Most effective promotional strategies for new products
   c. Performance level of individual territory sales
   d. Profit levels of all prescription pharmaceutical drugs

5. An electronic territory management system for sales representative is:-
   a. ADVANCE
   b. PRECISE
   c. PROFITS
   d. RE-SITE

Answers to Review Questions

1.   A

2.   A

3.   B

4.   A

5.   B

II. YOUR TERRITORIES AND CUSTOMERS

To really know your representatives territories you must be familiar with its people, districts, and records. How much do you need to know about the physicians and other healthcare professionals in your representatives territories? A lot, including:

* where they practice
* if they have multiple offices or clinics
* hospital affiliations
* their specialty or board certification
* their professional profile
* how often they should be visited
* how they fit into the territory itinerary cycle
* their buying history

The reason being, you as the District Manager need to have exceptional knowledge of each territory under your control. You will be responsible for inducting new representatives and training them in how to work and manage their territory effectively. You won't be able to do this if you are lacking in territory savvy.

Depending on how your pharmaceutical company structures its physician list, each sales representative will be allocated an area with a number of physicians, hospitals, clinics, and pharmacies that will form a territory. Usually this will have been organized by the previous territory representative prior to a new recruit. The number of physicians that the sales representative will be responsible for calling on will be determined by you the District Sales Manager or Regional Manager. The **promotional cycles** (period of time chosen by the marketing group) will also have an influence on the total] customers in each territory. The promotional cycle is determined by the marketing team to optimize the sales representative's contact with the health-care professionals in the territory. In managing a territory effectively, a top salesperson should consider the geography, the physician profiles, the extent of record keeping, and the system of planning.

You as the District Manager need to have exceptional knowledge of each territory under your control.

Objectives

The following objectives are provided to identify expected learning outcomes. When you finish this section, you should be able to:

1. Describe how planning and organization are determined by the sales territories.
2. List the information that should be kept in a physician profile.
3. Explain how accurate record keeping is critical for successful selling.
4. List some recommended methods for effective planning.

A. Geography

The geography of each territory will have a direct effect on their day to day

Size of territory may require travel, planning.

activities. You must know how far they will have to travel each day to make contact with your customers. You will also need to know it they have to live away from home for a period of time (days, week, etc). Traveling into rural areas may be more

> **KEY POINT**
> **The geography of a territory may affect the way that a sales representative organizes daily sales calls; the major objective is to minimize travel time and maximize selling time.**

demanding due to limitations of travel. For instance, they must book reservations for hotel rooms and rental cars (when

applicable), you must study and verify travel routes, and you must make sure that there is not a holiday during their planned travel. These are the types of limitations that may make traveling into these areas more challenging and time consuming.

Organized to maximize contact with important customers.

While a territory will have been organized by a previous representative, it may not suit the incoming person due to location of residence or other reasons, so adjustments may have to be made. The aim of the company is to provide the appropriate level of contact and service that is in line with the classification of the customer. When setting strategies, pharmaceutical companies first target high potential doctors, using the statistic that 20% of customers provide 80% of the business.

Second, doctors may also be identified for special VIP attention for political or professional reasons. Third, these customers should be visited as frequently as is practical. Therefore, the geographic layout of a territory can have an impact on how often calls are made on each type of customer. The major objective is to minimize travel time and maximize the face-to-face selling to high profile, targeted prescribers.

B. Physician Profile

A profile is usually built up over a period of time, beginning with the previous representative's records, if available and accurate. Previous records can save valuable time in helping to communicate effectively with each customer. Rapport, which refers to harmony or affinity, is important in creating long-term relationships with customers.

Profile information on physicians is available from various sources: data services (previously described), pharmacists, hospital staff, other sales colleagues, and local news. These sources will be especially important if a physician is new to a practice. Compiling a physician profile is an integral part of selling pharmaceutical products to the medical profession.

KEY POINT
Physician profiles should include types of patients seen, indications treated, therapies used most often system for obtaining appointments, hospital affiliation, which prescribing category the physician fits into size of the medical practice, and other important qualifiers of the physician.

Use outside sources to collect physicians' profile info

Physician profiles should include:

Information for physician profile

* the type of patients seen, indications treated, type of therapy used most often
* the system for obtaining an appointment
* the hospital affiliation, if any
* whether the customer is in the top 20% of prescribers, or has the potential to be
* the size of the medical practice and other professional interests
* drug therapy of choice for the specific area of treatment
* whether the physician is cautious or an early adopter of new medications
* how price-conscious the physician is
* the pharmacy of choice for prescriptions
* how receptive the physician is to pharmaceutical company meetings, representatives and samples

Record keeping, electronic or written is critical for success.

* what the personality style is
* personal information, such as family, hobbies, religion, club memberships, etc.

C. Record Keeping

Keeping accurate records about your territory and its customer is absolutely critical for effective selling. Is it unrealistic to assume that you will remember all of the details of a busy day. You must develop a habit of committing important information to a records system, regardless of whether it is electronic or written.

> **KEY POINT**
> **Accurate record keeping may be achieved using hand written notes or electronic means. Records of sales calls must be detailed and kept in a timely fashion to reduce the likelihood of forgetting valuable information.**

Laptop computers assist time management

Your record-keeping tools will be invaluable for you during your sales calls, whether they are provided by the company or from commercial sources, electronic call reporting helps maintain records and manage information. Of course, the aim of providing laptop computers for the pharmaceutical representative is to reduce record keeping time and increase selling time, develop and maintain call lists, adjust customer profiles as prescribing habits change, ensure easy access to a company database, and to provide a system for the sales representative to help him/her better manage their time.

D. Planning

"Nobody plans to fail, they fail to plan." This saying holds true for pharmaceutical sales representatives – planning should be a high priority in the life of a sales rep. You should always maintain a plan for: 1) you annual territory coverage, 2) your cycle itinerary, 3) physician, pharmacy, and hospital calls and 4) time management. If you plan well, you can maximize your productivity. Here are some suggestions to help you make their days more productive.

KEY POINT
Effective planning is imperative for successful selling. Ways to make their days more productive include planning on the evening before, avoiding heavy traffic times, and allowing adequate time between appointments.

Planning makes days more productive

1. Do not do their paperwork when they could be seeing physicians – do paperwork on their down time – not when the surgeries are in full swing.

2. Complete their daily plan on the evening before – make sure they have a contingency plan in the event of cancellations.

3. Advise them to avoid heavy traffic areas whenever possible and heavy traffic times – remember, many physicians work late.

4. Start early – get as many calls in before 10.00 AM as possible.

5. Show them where to park their car – work with parking attendants for easy access to parking spaces and future visits.

Tips to increase productivity

6. Ensure that your representatives do not book appointments too close together, especially if driving is involved. Allow enough time for commuting, parking, carrying out a pre-call analysis, and pharmacy call, if possible.

7. Get a good night's rest before their workdays – they will need their "edge" to maximize their sales.

Summary

The geography of a territory can have a major effect on the daily activities of the sales representative in charge of a territory. The sales representative must be aware of heavy traffic areas and times, the distances between calls, how long it will take to travel through the territory, and how long he/she will be away from home. The major objective is to minimize travel time and to maximize selling time.

Physician profiles are usually built over a period of time. Sales Representatives should develop extensive physician profiles to encourage rapport with the physician. This is very important in establishing long-term relationships with physicians.

Physician profiling is just one example of the record keeping that a Sales Representative must maintain. Record keeping helps the Sales Representative remember the details of the sales call. Keeping accurate records of the territory and its customers is critical for selling.

Planning is also a very important part of the sales representative's position, such as planning for annual territory coverage, cycle itinerary, and sales calls. It is also important to plan your time effectively. Planning will help keep the sales representative organized and on top of his/her territory.

Remember first impressions often last longest, the more knowledgeable you are about each representatives territory the more you are able to help them better perform their job, more quickly and consistently.

Review Questions

DIRECTIONS. Circle the letter corresponding to the correct answer for each question.

1. Important information for a physician profile includes all of the following, **except**:-
   a. Practice size and hospital affiliation
   b. Personal income level
   c. Personality style and hobbies
   d. Types of patients seen

2. The immediate reason for effective planning is to:-
   a. Avoid making sales calls on personal time
   b. Maintain accurate records
   c. Maximize productivity
   d. Reach customers before the competition does

3. The manager needs to have exceptional territory knowledge on the following except:-
   a. The geography of each territory
   b. The number of physician's in each territory
   c. The hospital affiliations of each territory
   d. The hospital affiliations of each physician

4. The purpose of record keeping is to:-
   a. To keep the boss happy
   b. Provide a system for reference in planning the call
   c. To record personal details of the physician
   d. None of the above

5. Physician profiles should include:-
   a. What the personality style is
   b. Types of patients seen, indications treated
   c. Drug therapy of choice
   d. How price conscious the physician is
   e. All of the above

Answers to Review Questions

1.   A

2.   C

3.   D

4.   B

5.   E

III. TIME MANAGEMENT

Time management is one of the most important skills that an effective District Sales Manager can possess. Time will always be one of your scarcest and important resources. The more time you have for your activities, the more effective you will be.

There is however, no simple solution to the problem of time management. Even the most experienced District Sales Managers never totally solve the time problem. But there are important benefits to you if you can accomplish more of the important tasks each day.

Time will always be one of your scarcest and important resources

Through controlling time you can exert more control over the events which influence your success. Time is highly perishable and unlike money it can't be saved or set aside for the future. Your use of time has an impact on everything you do as a District Sales Manager.

Objectives

The following objectives are provide to identify expected learning outcomes. When you finish this section you should be able to:

1. Define the five steps to effective time management.
2. Describe the method for allocating time for field visits.
3. Describe the benefits of managing time effectively.

Key Concepts

1. Time management is all about minimizing wasteful time and maximizing productive time.
2. The first step in time management is to find out where there is scope for improving your use of time.

Your use of time has an impact on everything you do as a District Sales Manager.

In addition to the many planning activities, the District Sales Manager must be able to accomplish the various tasks assigned to him/her as part of their overall responsibilities.

The District Sales Manager must be able to accomplish the various tasks assigned to him/her as part of their overall responsibilities.

The most important of these is the contact with sales rep's, either in the field on their territories, or at district meetings and training sessions. Here is a typical list of the activities that a District Sales Manager will handle:

* Field visits with sale reps
* Training new sales reps
* Working their own territory/accounts
* Meetings at the home office – marketing, medical, etc.
* Promotional cycle meetings
* Analyzing reports/processing mail
* Administrative duties – reports to home office, reports to sales reps, sales forecasting and trends, etc.

The problem that most District Sales Managers face is how to accomplish all of these activities in the time available.

The problem that most District Sales Managers face is how to accomplish all of these activities in the time available.

A. Five Steps to Effective Time Management

1) Understand your job responsibilities
2) Know how you are currently spending your time.
3) Establish priorities for each cycle in advance.
4) Determine "ideal" time allocations for each responsibility based on priorities
5) Manage each day as a separate unit in regard to the following:
   * Setting priorities
   * Recognizing potential time wasters
   * Planning for results

Understand your job responsibilities

Step 1.   Understand your job responsibilities

Regardless of whether you are new or experienced, it is important to periodically review your job description and all the activities you must carry out as a District Sales Manager. If you fully understand these, you can do some better planning and use your time more effectively. This will ensure that all of your activities and responsibilities can be handled adequately.

Step 2.   Know how you are currently spending your time

Unfortunately, very few managers do this well. In order to measure time and effectively allocate it, you cannot deal with job responsibilities alone – they are too broad. Time is used in terms of activities, and often many activities are necessary to carry out one responsibility.

You should periodically look back at your activities for the previous week, month, or cycle to see how you have used the time. By doing this, you can, monitor your time usage and make adjustments as needed. For example, a key responsibility is achieving sales objectives. To monitor time for this responsibility, look at specific activities, such as field visits with reps, analyzing reports, planning and conducting sales meetings, etc. All of these activities contribute to the performance of the responsibility.

Know how you are currently spending your time.

Step 3.   Establish priorities for each cycle in advance

As a District Sales Manager, you have many varying activities and responsibilities that must be accomplished over a period of time, yet they all have different time allocations. If you don't understand these priorities at the beginning of the period, you will not have a method for measuring how effectively they are being carried out. Equally important, make sure that you are allocating enough time for the important tasks.

Establish priorities for each cycle in advance.

Step 4.   Determine "ideal" time allocations for each responsibility

Allocate the appropriate time for performing those functions and activities. At least 70% of your time will be taken up by field work, your most important time consuming activity. Most of this time will be coaching, but some will be recruiting, selecting, and training new reps, working your own territory/ accounts (if you have them), field testing new detail aids and presentations, etc. Administrative work takes up considerable time, as do pre-cycle management and district meetings.

Determine "ideal" time allocations for each responsibility.

Step 5. Manage each day as a separate unit

Manage each day as a separate unit.

This is critical. You must not only consider long – range time allocation, but you must also focus on immediate priorities, which are constantly changing. You must also recognize and control time wasters – interruptions, delays, poor work habits, unforeseen problems and many others. If you can eliminate or at least minimize them, you will be using your time more productively.

Recognize and control time wasters – If you eliminate or at least minimize them, you will be using your time more productively.

Before you can do any kind of time management exercise, you need to know exactly how you are presently using your time. Use the following form (Where does your time go) in Figure 1. Be as objective as possible while filling out the form, to achieve maximum results.

Figure 1   WHERE DOES YOUR TIME GO?

ACTIVITY	CURRENT TIME (%)	PRIORITY	IDEAL TIME (%)
1. Observing field calls by sales reps and providing field coaching.			
2. Recruiting and providing initial training to new sales reps.			
3. Personally representing the company in key accounts, surveys, VIP or clinical meetings field work.			
4. Attending meetings for district managers.			
5. Preparing for and leading pre-cycle meetings.			
6. Analyzing or processing routine incoming mail.			
7. Responding by phone, memo or in person to queries, complaints or special requests that are non-routine in nature.			
8.			
9.			
TOTALS			

B. Allocating Time to Field Visits with Sales Reps

The amount of time that you allocate to work in the field with sales reps, is one of the most important activities that you will ever undertake. There are some good procedures that you can use as guidelines in the allocation of this time, lets take a look at them. First of all you have to allocate the amount of time that you spend with each rep according to his/her, level of competency. So first, classify each of the reps according to their competency level, for example:

"C" Reps = need maximum attention (new reps, weak performers, etc.)

"B" Reps = need average attention (good or average)

"A" Reps = need minimal attention (best people)

The next thing that you need to do, is to decide how much time you should spend with each of them, as a general rule it is a good suggestion to:

* Spend twice as much time with C reps than B reps
* Spend twice as much time with B reps than A reps

You will need to plan your objectives for each rep, and explain how you will accomplish them. In your planning you need to factor in other activities, such as:

* How many meetings must I conduct?
* How many meetings must I attend?
* Who will be taking vacation time during the period?
* Where will each rep be working, and how much time should I allow for travel?
* How much time do I have for administrative functions?

In order to demonstrate how important planning is to a District Sales Manager in relation to time, here is an exercise using the appropriate information in a specific country. For this example we will make several assumptions, the first being that a District Sales Manager spends at least 70 percent of his/her time in the field with his/her reps.

The amount of time that you allocate to work in the field with sales is one of the most important activities that you will ever undertake.

So first, classify each of the reps to their competency level.

A district manager spends at least 70 percent of his/her time in the field with his/her reps.

You should allocate your time with the reps according to their needs.

Number of working days in a year (5 x 52)			260
Less:	Holidays	10	
	Vacation	15	
	Meetings	<u>10</u>	<u>35</u>
Number of actual working days			225
Less 30% of time for office work			<u>67</u>
			158

This leaves 158 days available to work with reps to help them through coaching, counseling, etc.

As we mentioned in the previous exercise, you should allocate your time with the reps according to their needs.

The main job of a District Sales Manager is to train and coach the reps in most need of help.

You should plan to spend about twice as much time with the C's as you do with the B's, and about twice as much time with the B's as you do with the A's. Thus, for a 4 week period (20 work days), this works out to:

"A" reps – 2 days
"B" reps – 4 days
"C" reps – <u>8</u> days
                    14 days (70% of 20 work days)

Since the main job of a District Sales Manager is to train and coach the reps to produce sales, it is obvious that those in most need of help should receive the most attention from you. You also may ask the question, if the A's are so good, why spend time at all with them?

All reps need training even the best ones.

The answer is simple. In the chapter on coaching, you will see that all reps need training. Even the best ones can slip unconsciously into bad habits or neglect important skills. It's the job of the District Sales Manager to correct this situation. Additionally, even the best reps need:

* recognition of the good work they do

* information about what's happening in the home office or district, and

* someone to complain to

Furthermore, while working with your best people, you can pick up good methods and techniques they are using and pass them onto others.

A District Sales Manager has such limited time for field training and coaching of each representative so it is important to plan how much time to spend with each. Equally important is making maximum use of that time by setting the objectives you want to accomplish on each visit and the methods of achieving those objectives.

Set the objectives you want to accomplish on each visit and the methods of achieving those objectives.

One of the simplest and best ways to plan your daily work activities effectively, is by using a "To Do List". When you make up a "To Do List", what you need to do is list on a sheet of paper, all of the things that you need to do for that day. To the right of each item, put either and A, B, or C, in regard to their importance, the A in this case being the highest priority. Even if you only accomplish one "A" in the day, you know that you have completed the item of most importance today. We highly suggest that you make a new "To Do List", everyday, since the priorities change daily. There are many planners commercially available in paper format, or on the computer, which allow you to prioritize your daily activities as high, medium of low.

We highly suggest that you make a new "To Do List," everyday.

C.   Avoid Time Wasters

Last of all, the best way to plan your time effectively, is by avoiding what we referred to earlier as "Time Wasters". Here is a list of "Time Wasters." and an explanation of each.

* Procrastination – Putting off taking action, intentionally or by habit, usually because we are confused about which action to take first.

Best way to plan your time effectively, is by avoiding "Time Wasters".

* Having no clearly defined end result in mind – This leads to
  procrastination. It can also cause us to make false starts, to waste time and effort on superfluous activity, and to fail to see short cuts to getting the job done.

Our time is to be used efficiently on any project, we must contact those people who are vital to the process.

*   Failing to involve the right people – If our time is to be used efficiently on any project, we must contact the people who are vital to the process – to provide needed authority, make necessary decisions, provide needed information, or do some of the work through delegation. Otherwise, the project bogs down.

*   Not setting time limits and deadlines – both for starting a project and for bringing it to conclusion.

*   Failure to develop routine procedures – Some tasks are repetitive. By developing and following standard operating procedures they can be handled swiftly and easily each time they occur, often by a subordinate.

Some tasks can be handled more effectively by phone or mail from a central location.

*   Choosing the least efficient location – As one example, some tasks can be handled more effectively by phone or mail from a central location where you have a phone and your working files. Recognizing this can save you needless travel and waiting time. In some cases, choice of location can speed up a negotiating process because of its psychological effect on the people involved. Choosing the wrong location wastes your time.

Choosing the wrong location wastes your time.

*   Neglecting to combine or batch interrelated tasks – Failure to recognize and combine interrelated tasks can waste time by causing duplication of effort.

Remember, there is no way that we can increase the number of hours in a day, however, what we can increase is our effectiveness during these hours, through good time management.

Remember, there is no way that we can increase the number of hours in a day.

DAILY PLANNER

ACTIVITIES, PROJECTS, TASK, ASSIGNMENTS	TIME REQUIRED	DELEGATED	
		TO	FOLLOW UP CALLS
High Priority			
Medium Priority			
Low Priority			

Summary

This is one of the most important skills that an effective District Sales Manager can possess.

The more time you have to use in your productive activities, the more effective you will be.

There is no simple solution to the problem of time management, however through controlling time you can exert more control over the events which influence your success. You can accomplish much more for yourself with the same expenditures of effort. This is one of the most important skills that an effective District Sales Manager can possess. Regardless of whether you are a newly promoted District Sales Manager or an experienced one, time will always be one of your most important and rare resources. Time is constantly in motion and if you save a few minutes or hours, unless you use that time <u>immediately</u>, it is wasted and gone forever. Your use of time has an impact on everything you do as District Sales Manager. The more time you have to use in your productive activities, the more effective you will be.

Review Questions (Chapter IV)

DIRECTIONS. Circle the letter corresponding to the correct answer for each question.

1. Steps to effective time management include
   a. Know how you are currently spending your time
   b. Understand your job responsibilities
   c. Manage each day as a separate unit
   d. All of the above

2. Factors that affect time management include all of the following:-
   a. Controlling time impacts on everything you do
   b. Not setting deadlines and time limits
   c. Having an open door for staff discussions
   Answer True or False

3. The number of available working days for a District Sales Manager to work with reps is between.
   a. 170-180
   b. 150-160
   c. 180-190
   d. 160-170

4. a. C Reps need minimal attention
   b. B Reps need average attention
   c. A Reps need minimal attention
   d. All Reps need attention according to their needs.

Answers to Review Questions

1. D

2. A-True, B-True, C-True

3. B

4. D

V. RECRUITING AND HIRING

I. INTRODUCTION

Adding to or replacing staff is a very expensive exercise and is not a process to be taken lightly. Not hiring the right person for the job is exceptionally costly to all concerned, especially to the District Sales Manager who is carrying out the interviewing and selection process. You initiate the process by organizing a planned search.

Your success as a District Sales Manager will be determined more by the quality of the people you hire – 'Can do and will do' than virtually anything else.

In today's global, dynamic and ever changing environment you can't afford to make a mistake in your selection. If you agree that the definition of management is 'getting profitable results through others', then you had better make a habit of hiring 'competent salespeople', it has been estimated that the cost to a company of hiring and training a new sales representative during the first year on the job to be between $25,000 and $90,000. Add this cost to the potential sales loss due to the poor quality of selection and the period of time having vacant territories, you can easily see the necessity of hiring the right people for the job.

Objectives

These objectives are included here to help you focus on expected learning outcomes. Once you have completed this section you should be able to:-

1.   Describe three ways for finding potentially strong candidates.
2.   Describe the Do's & Don'ts of conducting interviews.
3.   Describe the characteristics and capabilities required for a Sales Representative.
4.   Define the five legal guidelines stated in the text.
5.   Describe the questions you may use in checking references from employees.

Replacing staff is a very expensive exercise and is not a process to be taken lightly.

Success as a District Sales Manager will be determined more by the quality of the people you hire – 'Can do and will do'.

Make a habit of hiring 'competent salespeople'

Key Concepts

1. It is the District Sales Manager's responsibility to hire salespeople who:-

    *   If experienced can demonstrate that they have the knowledge/ skills and attitude required.

Remember enthusiasm is contagious – so is lack of it!

2. If inexperienced can demonstrate that they have the ability to learn, retain and utilize product knowledge/skills as required supported by a positive mental attitude.

    *   Can satisfy you that they are the best qualified to be able to more than meet the standard required.

3. Will be able to fit into a team and enhance it by them becoming a valuable contributor to the team results.

4. Can demonstrate enthusiasm and conviction that they are a winner.

'The greatest problem in the world today is apathy, but really I couldn't care less.'

Source Unknown

A. Steps in Recruiting & Hiring

1. Develop an appropriate job description and required competencies that will provide you with a source of applicants that meet the job requirements – specify the candidate in relation to the job.

2. Recruit a significant number of qualified candidates.

3. Develop a selection criteria screening out unqualified applicants by reśumé analysis.
    a) Telephone evaluation
    b) Brief personal interview
    c) Applications and reśumé analysis

4. Analyze remaining reśumé/applications and plan your interviews.

5. Conduct the interview the with the candidates to determine who meets the desired qualifications.

6. Select the candidates who are best qualified to do the job, (reduce list to 3 probables).

7. Check references conduct a second interview accompanied by another person (your boss, another District Sales Manager, a qualified Human Resources person)

8. Discuss your findings and rate 1,2 or 3 in order of preference.

9. Select the candidate who is best qualified.

10. Check references to verify information provided before making the job offer.

    * These steps should still apply even if using the 'Target Selection' method.

' I once took a four year course on positive thinking and at the end of three years I didn't know whether I should continue the course or give it up'.

Ronnie Corbett

Step I.   Develop A Job Description

A Guide to a Pharmaceutical Representative's Role in the Pharmaceutical Industry

Many people have a misconception of what a pharmaceutical sales representative's job entails.   A workday does not involve moving freely from one doctor's office to another, engaging their attention as required to promote a product. This job is demanding, interesting, varied and rewarding. It involves extensive planning, initiative, and hard work. The following section will describe the basic job responsibilities as well as the attributes that make a top salesperson.

Typical job description for pharmaceutical sales representative.

A. Pharmaceutical Sales Representatives: Job Description

Job descriptions for pharmaceutical sales representatives will vary among companies. However, a typical job description that may be used to attract new recruits is:

TITLE: Sales Representative, Sales Specialist, Associate, Territory Manager, etc

REPORTS TO: District Sales Manager/Area Manager

RESPONSIBILITIES:

1. To create and develop the
    maximum profitable sales of
    company products which may
    reasonably be achieved in the
    assigned territory through complete
    and aggressive coverage of all
    contacts and outlets.

> **KEY POINT**
> **Sales representatives
> must maximize territory
> sales and promote their
> company products**

2. To build customer goodwill and gain understanding and acceptance of
    company products and policies.

A satisfactory performance is
reached when total sales volume within
the **territory** shows an overall annual
increase, meeting or exceeding targets
set by district managers. Also, there
should be a balance among promoted
products and all customers within the
territory should be covered on a regular

> **KEY POINT**
> **Sales representatives
> are considered successful
> if the annual sales for their
> territory meet or
> exceed targets set by
> district managers.**

**Success is
Reaching district
targets**

basis. The sales representative is a vital link between the company and the
customer for the prompt and accurate transmission of information which
can solve problems, satisfy concerns, assist the research function, or provide
valuable market data. The company's interests muxt always be furthered in
the territory.

**Sales rep is link
between company,
customers**

Whether the customer is a private physician or managed
care clinic or hospital, maintaining accurate records on
each customer is an important responsibility.
Responsibilities of the sales representative include being
thoroughly familiar with the medical specialty, key
decision makers and their personalities, buying history, community and
professional connections, best time for sales calls, and the customers'
reaction to previous presentations. A sales call to each customer must be
fully planned, with frequency of visits and specific objectives decided on by
the salesperson in consultation with the district manager.

**Accurate records,
notes must be
kept on each
customer**

**Sales calls are
planned**

Reports, other documents are required

Sales representatives are also responsible for other documentation that is equally important, such as weekly planners, expenses, company forms, territory reports, customer orders, complaints, responses, and requests.

B. Attributes of the Top Sales Representative

Certain personal qualities are expected

The person who joins a pharmaceutical company will be expected to have the following qualities: sincerity, empathy, initiative, honesty, integrity, persistence, and a positive attitude toward the company, its products, its customers and it future. Since he or she will be judged in these following areas, a top sales person must excel in all areas of the Wheel of Success: business knowledge, industry knowledge, company-specific

---

KEY POINT
Top sales representatives excel in business, industry, company, and product knowledge, as well as selling skills. All these qualities are supported by a positive attitude that drives the Wheel of Success.

---

knowledge, product knowledge, selling skills and a positive attitude. Sales representatives are often judged in these areas.

The Wheel of Success

Knowledge, skills attitude drive the Wheel of Success

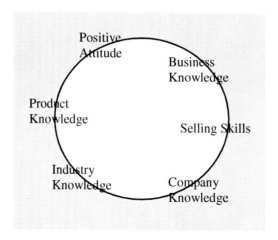

Business knowledge. This involves a general understanding of the language of business, such as profits, cash flow, overheads, marketing, budgeting and others. While some may choose to enroll in a formal business curriculum, it is also possible to become knowledgeable by reading major newspapers and business or trade journals. Familiarity with the business environment of your customers will allow you to translate product features into economic benefits for them. This is very important when dealing with managed care customers. You must be aware of how their cash flow, profits, and budgeting play a role in your sales success.

Business terms, knowledge of customer's environment

Industry knowledge. There is considerable information available regarding the evolving healthcare industry, how your customers must fit into the new systems, what new challenges your company must meet, and how the competitors are meeting them. A top salesperson must keep abreast of trends, statistics, pricing, research and developments within their industry, including customers, competitors, and related businesses.

Evolving health-care industry and new challenges

Company knowledge. Most companies provide thorough training for new sales associates, including both product-oriented education and information about the company itself. It is important to learn the financial and technological history, reputation and market share, competitors, formal and informal structure, policies, mission, and development plans. Strengths of the company and the reputation of the company should be stressed in sales calls, when appropiate.

Company's history reputation, mission

Product knowledge. In order to successfully represent a product, it will be necessary to know all aspects of the product, from design and development, to the manufacturing process and marketing of the product. The company has an interest in training its sales force to be fully knowledgeable in their products, including hands-on use of delivery systems and devices, if needed. It is also important to be equally informed about competitors' products in order to overcome customer objections. Be warned that many universities and healthcare organizations are training their phyicians to test and scrutinize your knowledge – make sure that the product information that you provide is up-to-date and accurate!

Full knowledge of product, from design to delivery

Effective selling skills

Selling skills. A top salesperson should possess certain personality traits which will communicate trust, knowledge, and confidence to the customer. In addition, a sales presentation should reflect planning, organization , and respect for the customer's time. The steps for achieving this while accomplishing the objectives of the call will be presented in the section titled The Sales Call.

Positive attitude leads to action, success

Positive attitude/action. A positive attitude allows a sales representative to elicit positive actions – after all, a positive attitude without any positive action does not sell anything! For instance, if a sales representative with a positive attitude does not get out into the field to sell, he or she will not be considered successful. A positive attitude that leads to positive actions is the main driving force behind the 'Wheel of Success.' Probably the most common fault in selling is a weakness in attitude and action – the lack of a strong positive attitude often results in disappointing sales. If the positive attitude is strong and there is the will to use it, the process will run smoothly to the benefit of the representative and company.

C. Professional Conduct

First impressions should reflect professionalism

An old adage that is important to remember: "You never get a second chance to make a first impression." Therefore, planning a sales presentation means that you need to spend enough time to ensure that your message reflects professionalism. This requires considerable preparation.

Six Ps

Remember the six Ps:

    Proper

    Planning

    Prevents

    Particularly

    Poor

    Presentation

> **KEY POINT**
> A professional sales representative knows the product, is resourceful, maximizes opportunities, is proficient at fact-finding, develops expertise, utilizes selling strategies, uses a systematic approach to selling, is industrious, is orderly, develops negotiating skills, strives for achievement, and expands his/her knowledge.

How well you carry out your sales presentations and how successful you are will be determined by your professionalism. In the past, the term "professional" signified either a person who had attended a university or college and had acquired a degree in medicine, law, science or education, or a person who was paid for playing a sport. Today, however, we use the term PROFESSIONAL when referring to how well a person performs in their chosen job rather than what that chosen job is. Virtually every industry is spending millions of dollars annually to improve the professional image of their employees in areas such as attitude, expertise, skills, experience, ethics, customer serive, knowledge, habits and workplace diversity.

Professional means how one performs in a chosen job

A description of qualities important for a successful professional pharmaceutical sales representative is presented below. At the end of this section you will find a rating scale for self evaluation.

Qualities of a PROFESSIONAL

P = Product knowledge. To the customer, a professional sales representative should be an authority on the company he or she represents, the products being promoted, and all relevant competitors. More often than not, the customer depends on the sales representative for technical advice, marketing information, and industry news. This is even more important for the managed care customer.

P is for product knowledge

R = Resourcefulness. The professional should take advantage of the resources that are provided by the company: sales reports, strategy recommendations, customer date, business or professiona journals, sales aids, and referrals.

R is for resourcefulness

O = Opportunism. The sales professional sees objections raised by the customer as opportunities to provide information and capitalize on the situation prior to making the sale. Although there will be some reluctance encountered, a persistent representative should continue calling on tough customers until a successful relationship is established.

O is for opportunism

F = Fact-finding. The professional does not accept things at face value, but will probe to prove that facts are supported by evidence.

F is for fact-finding

E is for expertise	**E = Expertise.** " An amateur practices until he or she gets things right and then stops," but the professional "practices until he/she never gets things wrong."
S is for selling strategy	**S = Selling strategy.** The professional ensures that their presentation skills are sharpened by role play and self analysis.
S is for systematic	**S = Systematic approach.** The professional has an approach to selling which utilizes planning, preparation and evaluation to optimize efficiency and effectiveness.
I is for initiative	**I = Initiative.** The professional works very hard to achieve results, which may require starting early and finishing late.
O is for orderliness	**O = Organization.** Prior to a sales visit, the professional representative should be rehearsed, organized and ready to handle any anticipated situation.
N is for negotiating	**N = Negotiating skills.** The needs of the customer must be identified, anticipated, and met. The sales professional is both an advocate for the customer and a representative of the company, and is successful at reaching a mutual benefit for the two.
A is for achievement	**A = Achievement.** A love of selling and a desire for accomplishments are components of the positive attitude which drives the 'Wheel of Success.' A top salesperson enjoys competition and seeks a winning outcome.
L is for lateral thinking	**L = Lateral thinking.** A lateral thinker is not satisfied with the current level of knowledge, but actively seeks to expand his or her thinking process through related reading, audio cassettes, self-study, seminars, and professional networking.
	Now take a moment to rate yourself on these qualifies. Score yourself against these qualities on a scale of 1 (low) to 10 (high).

Representative Professional Self Assessment Scale

Rate yourself: from 1 to 10 for each quality, then add all scores for your total.

Low   1 2 3 4 5 6 7 8 9 10   High

P   **Product Knowledge**

R   **Resourcefulness**

O   **Opportunism**

F   **Fact-finding**

E   **Expertise**

S   **Selling strategy**

I   **Industriousness**

O   **Orderliness**

N   **Negotiating skills**

A   **Achievement**

L   **Lateral thinking**

Total:

If you have a total of 96 to 120, you have all the qualities of a top sales representative!

If you score below seven or below on any of items listed above this element of professionalism needs attention.

Summary

Sales representatives are responsible for creating and developing the maximum sales of products within a defined territory. They must also build customer goodwill and gain understanding and acceptance of company products and policies. The company's interests in the territory should always be considered and furthered.

Success for the sales representative comes when annual sales for the territory reach or exceed target sales volumes. This success depends on the attributes of the sales representative. Successful representatives have business, industry, company-specific and competitive product knowledge. They also have selling skills and a positive attitude. Successful sales representatives also are capable of professional conduct, which includes essential qualities: product knowledge, resourcefulness, opportunism, fact-finding ability, expertise, selling strategies, systematic approaches to sales, industrious and orderly, negotiating skills, achievement goals, and lateral thinking skills.

> *Amateurs practice until they get things right and stop, professionals practice until they never get things wrong.*

Review Questions (Chapter V)

DIRECTIONS. Circle the letter corresponding to the correct answer for each question.

1. It is the District Sales Managers responsibility to:-
   a. Recruit and hire experienced Sales Representatives
   b. Hire candidates who have worked current vacant territories
   c. Hire representatives who sold similar products with difference companies.
   d. Select the candidates who are best qualified to do the job.

2. The definition of effective management is:-
   a. Hiring the best salespeople in the business. To get results.
   b. Having the lowest turnover of salespeople
   c. Getting profitable results through others
   d. None of the above

3. In the PROFESSIONAL rating scale, the R stands for _____ and the N stands for _____.
   a. Realistic and neat
   b. Reinforcing and notable
   c. Relational and natural
   d. Resourcefulness and negotiating

4. The responsibility of a sales professional is to:-
   a. Maximize distribution of the company's products throughout the sales territory.
   b. Meet or exceed target sales goals set by the district manager.
   c. Meet personal income goals and thereby meet company goals.
   d. Replace competitors products on customers' shelves.

5. The Wheel of Success as a sales representative includes all of the following, **except**
   a. Aggressive attitude
   b. Business knowledge
   c. Product knowledge
   d. Selling skills

Answers to Review Questions

1.   D

2.   C

3.   D

4.   A

5.   A

Step II. Recruit Qualified Applicants

INTRODUCTION

Recruiting and hiring qualified applicants is not an easy task however it can be very rewarding. Do not make the mistake of many managers who have hired the 'best' of a bad bunch of applicants because the thought of repeating this tiring, time consuming exercise did not appeal. It is better to have anyone covering a territory than have a vacant territory, - wrong decision.

Objectives

These objectives are included here to help you focus on expected learning outcomes. Once you have completed this section you should be able to:-

1.   Describe the five more common recruiting sources.
2.   List the three screening methods for applicants.
3.   Describe the types of questions that should be used during the interviews.

Key Concepts

1.   Select the candidates who are the best qualified.
2.   Then only hire the candidates who can do and will do the job.

Recruiting Sources:-

Here are suggested recruiting sources. They differ in effectiveness from area to area but these are the more common ones to consider.

A.   Business Contacts

Used with discretion, your business contacts can be a good network for spreading the word about the position you have open.

The key is "discretion". Some of your contacts refer only candidates who, they believe, fulfill the requirements as you have explained them. Others may play upon your friendship and send poorly qualified relatives or family friends, hoping to pressure you into hiring them.

If using business contacts the key is discretion.

Think twice before you invite any key business influences or customers to send you candidates.

B.   Company Personnel:

Other managers and sales representatives in your company may know people who would make good sales representatives. Company personnel are likely to be a good source for internal referrals and often they will recommend good candidates.

Company personnel are likely to be a good source for internal referrals

C.   University or other School Placement Offices:

These can be good sources for continuous recruiting efforts, It's a good idea to maintain your relationship with these people if they prove to be helpful.

D.   Classified Advertisements:

Advertising is a good way for obtaining many applicants in a hurry. It should not replace other sources nor be used as a sole source.

* Trade publications are excellent to use when you are seeking an experienced pharmaceutical sales representative.
* Newspapers are a good source for obtaining a large number of applicants but those applicants will require heavy screening.

E.   Personnel Agencies:

Those who specialize in pharmaceutical sales or sales in general can be helpful. Some are good but overall quality is variable. Use care.

FINALLY, AS YOU DEVELOP VALUABLE SOURCES ON YOUR OWN, THEY ARE WELL WORTH REMEMBERING FOR FUTURE REFERRALS.

Step III. Screen Applicants

SCREENING METHODS

A.   TELEPHONE EVALUATION

B.   BRIEF PERSONAL INTERVIEW

C.   APPLICATION AND RESUME ANALYSIS

Step IV.   Plan the Interview

GUIDELINES FOR PLANNING THE INTERVIEW

Candidate's Name _____

Date of Interview _____

Relaxer _____

A good guide to what will be done in the future is what has been done in the past.

A. Warning Signs

(Any danger signal, serious concern, information

that needs to be further clarified and evaluated):

Questions to ask

* Frequent job changes? How? Where?

* Lack of progress, inconsistent career path? When?

* Recent failure in own business? What?

* Over-qualified or earnings too high? Who? Why?

* Possible personal or financial problems? _____

* Inconsistencies, missing information,
  conflicting dates?

B. Education

* Completed program of study? **Questions to ask**

* Productive or career-related summer jobs? How? Where?

* Major field of study consistent with career? When?

* Significant achievements and activities? What?

* Education expenses partially or fully earned? Who? Why?

* Grades satisfactory? _____

* Sciences studied?

C. Work History

* Experience compatible with Sales Representative position?
* Past reporting relationships satisfactory?
* Length of experience meets Sales Representative qualifications?
* Acceptable reasons for leaving prior employers?
* Achieved results in previous positions?

Questions to ask

How? Where?

When?

What?

Who? Why?

D. Skills and knowledge

* Degree of public/sales experience meets Sales Representative qualifications?
* Pharmaceutical/healthcare knowledge meets Sales Representative qualifications?
* Has necessary background (chemistry, biology, or other required knowledge base)?

Questions to ask

How? Where?

When?

What?

Who? Why?

Skills can be taught, knowledge can be learned.

E. Motivation and attitude

* Has demonstrated hard work, initiative?
* Quality of relationships with previous co-workers, supervisors?
* Has shown aggressiveness?
* Indications of being organized, capable of self-management?
* Apparent desire to succeed?

Questions to ask

How? Where?

When?

What?

Who? Why?

Motivation is internal attitude within

If it is meant to be? Then it is up to me!

Talbot Smith

Arrange the Interview

Prior to conducting recruiting and hiring interviews there are several things that need to be completed.

Suspend all phone calls

a) Select an appropriate venue preferably a small suite in a suitable hotel suspending all phone calls and any other suspected interruptions.

Allow an appropriate amount of time

b) Schedule your appointments allowing enough time for each interview so there is adequate time to create a friendly environment for the interviewee to relax and feel comfortable.

Use time judiciously.

c) To save the District Sales Manager valuable time, screening interviews may be handled at recruitment offices by the head hunter of choice or by a qualified Human Resource person.

District Sales Manager does final screening.

d) The final screening should be performed by the District Sales Manager after he/she has had an opportunity to analyze the applicants resumés to determine if they meet the education and employment requirements and have the qualifications to do the job.

Eliminate unsuitable applicants.

e) If the resumé and applications do not meet the standards set then they should be eliminated from any further interviews.

Step V. Interview Candidates

GUIDELINES FOR CONDUCTING AN EFFECTIVE INTERVIEW

1. Follow the plan that you have made for the interview.

    Follow your plan.

2. Ask open-ended questions; primarily those requiring many words to answer. Be sure to listen carefully to the answers. Do not ask leading questions that "give away" the answer. An example: "We need the kind of person who is self-motivated and dependable, a person who will work all day making calls. Are you that kind of person?"

    Ask open ended questions.

3. Be persistent. Follow up on any information given by the candidate that is incomplete, questionable or unclear. Determine the meaning by using an open-ended questions such as "In what ways was it difficult?" or with direct questions like, "When exactly did you have your last position?"

    Resistance can't live with persistence.

4. Maintain a receptive attitude throughout. Your facial expressions, gestures, posture should convey approval, acceptance, interest and understanding.

    Be receptive.

5. Avoid any signal of disapproval toward unfavorable responses. Remain neutral; avoid excessive approval also.

    Remain neutral.

6. Be brief and businesslike in taking notes. If you want to note an unfavorable item, wait until you move to a new subject before writing.

    Be business like.

7. Bridge from one subject to another by commenting on the subject just covered, and setting up the next. For example, "Conducting hospital exhibits must have been interesting. Tell me about your other selling activities."

    Use appropriate bridging questions.

8. Speak naturally and slowly, smile often, react warmly and be friendly.

    Smile and convey friendliness.

GUIDELINES FOR CONDUCTING AN
EFFECTIVE INTERVIEW (cont)

Keep your mind open

9. Keep an open mind while interviewing. If you make up your mind that one of the early candidates is the right person, it will interfere with your objectivity during later interviews.

Avoid biases.

10. Do not let you personal biases or feelings influence your reactions or thoughts during the interview.

85%/15%

11. The candidate should do most of the talking. Avoid dominating the interview.

No need to sell your company.

12. Don't try to sell your company to the candidate. This is an interview of the candidate.

APPEARANCE

SKILLS

ATTITUDE

WORK HISTORY

EDUCATION

EXPERIENCE

INITIATIVE

CONSISTENCY

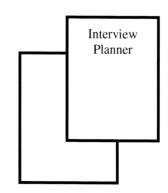

Interview Planner

```
* Rule of Thumb when interviewing
  Interviewee 85% of the talking
  Interviewer 15% of the talking
```

EFFECTIVE USE OF QUESTIONS DURING INTERVIEWS

OPEN-ENDED QUESTIONS are preferred because they often provide more information, and the answers sometimes divulge facts and feelings that you would not have expected.

DIRECT QUESTIONS (requiring a short factual answer, or a 'yes' or 'no') are useful, but too many limit information and impose too tight a control of the interview. Direct questions are good for uncovering specific, details and concerns.

Different type of *OPEN-ENDED* questions help you assess attitudes, feelings, and to uncover significant facts about an applicant.

Open questions begin with the words

Who

What

Where

When

How

Why

TYPE	EXAMPLE
* Feeling, thinking	- How do you feel about a career in pharmaceutical selling?
* Superlative	- What did you like best (or worst) about your manager at Wholesale Drug Co.?
* Motivational	- Why did you leave your employment at the laboratory? What are you career goals?
* Inside Story	- What were the circumstances that caused you to leave the institute prior to graduation?
* Consistency	- What was it you said earlier about......
* Loyalty	- How do you feel about your present company?.

Direct questions are designed to get a Yes/No answer.

A person who has little or no loyalty for their past employer may have none for your company

Step VI. Select the Best Qualified Applicant

In the following text is a list of Do's and Don'ts to consider that may assist you in conducting successful interviews.

Do – Relax your applicant

* Put your interviewee at ease by establishing rapport – using "small talk" about how the applicant was able to find the interview location, current state of the weather, sporting events etc.

* Prepare a checklist of questions preferably using open questions to find out about their motivations, and what each candidate wants from the job. Open questions start with the words. Who, What, Where, When Why and How.

Ask questions that verify:-

Their education history

Their work history

Skills and knowledge information

Motivation/attitude information

* Do ask questions that verify
   a) Their education history
   b) Their work history
   c) Skills and knowledge information
   d) Motivation/attitude information

Areas that may need further clarification and evaluation.

* Listen attentively and pay attention to the answers you receive.

* Commence with open questions that are non-specific and then move to specific questions.

* Determine what they know about your company and products and if they did their homework before the interview.

Don'ts - First check with your Legal Department and or Human Resources Department regarding the subjects that can't or should not be discussed. Including, sex, (gender), age, religion, race, politics, marital status, handicaps, etc.

EXERCISE:

Applicant's Name _____

FINAL CHECKLIST/SUMMARY

This is your final "countdown" for each applicant. Basically, this checklist is intended to help you to analyze the total picture of the applicant. It also asks some serious additional questions that you should answer yourself before making a hiring decision.

OVERALL APPLICANT RATING

☐ Outstanding   ☐ Questionable qualifications
☐ Above average   ☐ Eliminate from consideration

	Yes	No
Are there any "unsatisfactory" responses that can't be resolved or accepted?	☐	☐
Does the applicant have the required experience and employment history (progress, results, consistency, earning, responsibility) to do the job?	☐	☐
Has the applicant demonstrated efficient work habits and effective interpersonal relationships?	☐	☐
Are the applicant's educational background and academic record adequate for this position?	☐	☐
Does the applicant have the required skills and knowledge for the job?	☐	☐
Does the applicant's motivational qualifications and needs fit the job and work environment?	☐	☐
Are there any concerns remaining that have not been sufficiently probed, discussed, or satisfactorily answered?	☐	☐
Does the applicant possess the personality, appearance, and communication skills to handle the job?	☐	☐
Has most of the information you have obtained been verified with reference checks?	☐	☐

Are there any "unsatisfactory" responses that can't be resolved or accepted?

Are the applicant's educational background and academic record adequate for this position?

Has most of the information you have obtained been verified with reference checks?

Step VII.   Check References

HOW TO CHECK REFERENCES

You must verify the facts about the candidate's past work record.

After you make your selection but before you make an offer, check the candidate's references. At this point, you have selected the candidate who seems best suited for the job. This is only a tentative selection; your final decision will depend on reference checks to verify information that the candidate has given to you. You must verify the facts about the candidate's past work record.

No matter how impressed you may be with a candidate, this step is required to develop a true picture. Applicants can be expected to present themselves in a highly favorable light. Who can blame them? In their eagerness to impress, they may substitute fiction for fact by:-

* Adapting their work histories to their own favor. This is done by almost everyone. Some, however, bend the truth beyond recognition.

* Covering up. Unfavorable facts in the work history can be concealed by expanding employment dates to drop out a job that will provide a poor reference. People may claim higher sales (and salaries) than they actually achieved.

* Falsifying. Applicants who deliberately lie about qualifications may claim "two years of sales experience" when the work was actually confined to the office, requiring only an occasional outside service call.

Discrepancies can be uncovered only by checking business and personal references.

Such discrepancies can be uncovered only by checking business and personal references.

Checks with previous employers may be made in three ways:

1. **By mail.** This is the poorest method, but some company policies require it. Employers are reluctant to put in writing any information of a negative character, if they reply at all.

HOW TO CHECK REFERENCES (cont)

2.   **In person.** A personal call on the applicant's immediate previous supervisor is a desirable method. If the employer is in the area and can be reached easily, the time spent in making the call will be well worthwhile.

3.   **By telephone.** Distance and lack of time frequently make the personal call impractical, or even impossible. The telephone check is an efficient and practical method that gives excellent results. If approached properly, previous supervisors will tell you things that they would never put in writing.

Begin you reference check by establishing rapport, identifying yourself and explaining the reason for your call. Then ask the previous employer the following questions:-

* What were the candidate's dates of employment?
* What was the candidate's job?
* What was the candidate's salary?
* How was the candidate's work attendance?
* How was the candidate's work compared to other employees?
* How was the candidate's strong points/weaknesses?
* In what respects could the candidate improve?
* Why did the candidate leave?
* Would you rehire the candidate?
* How good a salesperson is the candidate?

Of course, this is only asked if the employer you are talking with is the person who supervised the applicant in a sales job. If the employer supervised the candidate in a job totally different from a sales position, describe the Sales Representative's position briefly and ask the employer if he/she thinks the applicant would be successful in this type of work. Say for example, "The job (applicant's name) has applied for requires the person to be energetic, calling on physicians and hospital personnel and detailing our products to retail and wholesale pharmaceutical outlets. How do you think (applicant's name) would do at this kind of job?

Do not contact a candidate's current employer unless you have the person's specific permission to do so!

In what respects could the candidate improve?

Why did the candidate leave?

Would you rehire the candidate?

Concern Items

Work History

Motivation

Education

Knowledge

Skills

Attitude

It is a very expensive and time consuming exercise, recruiting and hiring and then training and developing new staff.

Hire representatives that have the right drive and attitude that 'can do and will do the job.'

HOW TO CHECK REFERENCES (cont)

If you have a concern item to bring up, use a "leading" question that provides direction. For example, "One of the things that troubles me slightly is (concern). Have you observed that also?"

If you have received a completely favorable report from the employer, then ask one last leading question to be sure that nothing has been left unsaid. An example, "Obviously, you think that (applicant's name) is a good employee, and I do too. Assuming we hire (applicant's name), how do you think I can be of most help to them?" Then note any significant answers on the application form.

Once the candidate passes these final tests, you are ready to make the job offer. This is the easiest and most pleasant task of all.

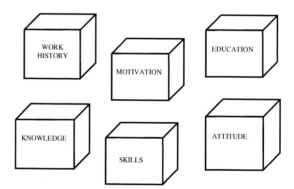

SUMMARY

It is a very expensive and time consuming exercise, recruiting and hiring and then training and developing new staff. Today's global marketplace demand's that you employ the best possible Sales Representatives that you can attract to your company, then in turn they need to stay at least three years for your investment to be returned. It has been estimated that the cost of advertising, recruiting, selecting and training a new representative to a company can cost between $25.000 and $90,000. Turn over of staff depletes profits so – hire representatives that have the right drive and attitude that 'can do and will do the job that they will be paid for.

Review Questions (Chapter V)

DIRECTIONS. Circle the letter corresponding to the correct answer for each question.

1. Items for concern:-
    a. Education, previous experience, motivation, knowledge
    b. Previous experience, education, knowledge, motivation
    c. Motivation, knowledge, previous experience, education
    d. Work history, motivation, knowledge, selling skills

2. Open questions begin with the words:-
    a. Who, what, where, when, how, should
    b. What, should, where, when, why, now
    c. Who, where, what, when, how, why
    d. Should, how, where, when, where, what

3. Direct questions
    a. Too many limit information and impose a tight control
    b. Not enough limit information
    c. Relax the applicant and let them speak freely
    d. Are good for uncovering general information

4. a. Show signs of disapproval if warranted.
    b. Open questions should be used to encourage the candidate to open up and relax
    c. Open questions lets the candidate give you their life story
    d. Your facial expressions and gestures should convey disapproval of unfavorable responses, interests, acceptance and understanding, business like approach, approval, friendliness, acceptance, business like approach

Answers to Review Questions

1. D

2. C

3. C

4. B

VI. COMMUNICATIONS

I. DEFINITION OF COMMUNICATION

If we want to learn how to communicate effectively, we need to first define what we mean by communication. There are many theories about communication, but usually communication is defined as the process whereby one person (sender) sends a message to a specific person or group (receiver). We as managers must understand and convey to our Sales Representatives and district team members:

* The Importance of Communications
* Communications Principles
* The Manager's Role in Communications
* Roadblocks to Good Communications
* Effective Communications Techniques
* What You Can do to be an Effective Communicator

There are many theories about communication, but usually communication is defined as the process whereby one person (sender) sends a message to a specific person or group (receiver).

Objectives

These learning objectives will help you focus your attention on learning outcomes. After completing this section you should be able to:

1. Discuss the importance of communications
2. Describe the elements of communication principles
3. Define the manager's role in communications
4. Describe the roadblocks to effective communications.

The intent and content of the communications need to be understood to be effective.

Key Concepts

1. Communication is a two way process.
2. The skill of communication is not inherent it needs to be developed and utilized appropriately.
3. The intent and content of the communications need to be understood to be effective.

A. The Importance of Communication

Communications can often be referred to as the bond that holds all organizations together.

Communication is one of the most important activities of our daily lives. We have seen wars, strife, governments fall, all because of poor Communications. In this chapter we will explore what you need to know about communications, not only to be an effective District Sales Manager, but to be effective in any management position. Communications can often be referred to as the bond that holds all organizations together. It has been often said that communications is the single greatest influence on the effectiveness of an organization. Communications deserve a lot more effort, attention, and importance, than they usually receive in an organization. Communications represent a lot of money to organizations, the District Sales Manager's ability to communicate effectively with his or her sales people can increase the district's effectiveness.

Communications is the single greatest influence on the effectiveness of an organization.

Diagram:

Sender _____> Receiver
$\qquad\qquad\qquad$ Message

The process used in transmitting the message involves a stimulation or response from the receiver.

Sender <_____>Receiver

In order to communicate effectively, we also need to listen effectively.

So for communication to be effective, it really needs to be a two way process. One of the basics that we often forget is, in order to communicate effectively, we also need to listen effectively. If we are not good listeners and do not have good listening skills, our communication effectiveness will be diminished. Another problem that frequently occurs with listening, is that we also assume that others are listening intently to what we are saying, and we are often wrong. Therefore it is imperative that both the sender and the receiver are good listeners.

Therefore it is imperative that both the sender and receiver are good listeners.

There are things that hamper our listening effectiveness, one of them is our frame of reference.

B. How Frame of Reference Affects Communications

Everyone sees life and people and events from their own viewpoint. The factors which influence our interpretation of these matters make up what is known as a frame of reference. We evaluate every happening against our experience, ideals, attitudes, goals, obligations and beliefs.

When we are asked to be objective or to make impartial decisions, we are sometimes being asked to do the impossible. We cannot disassociate ourselves from our frame of reference. Doctors, scientists, and research people all admit that they like certain people more than others, that they prefer to associate with people who are like themselves, that personal feelings often cloud their judgement in important matters.

C. Communications Principles

For communication to be effective, there are various elements that need to be considered.

* The subject matter or topic, (basic or advanced)
* The media that will deliver the communication
* Formal or informal presentation
* The exact response anticipated by the communicator

Let's look at each of these principles in more detail, and explain them. No matter how basic or advanced our message is, it always makes good sense to keep it short and simple. As the old cliché goes; use the principle KISS, Keep It Short and Simple. However regardless of how simple we keep our message, there will always be some people who will make it complicated.

> **K**eep
> **I**t
> **S**hort &
> **S**imple

The factors which influence our interpretation are known as a frame of reference.

Personal feelings often cloud our judgement in important matters.

It always makes good sense to keep it short and simple.

What is very important in all our communications, is how our audience interprets and understands the messages.

What is very important in all our communications, is how our audience interprets and understands the messages. Communication is defined by how it is interpreted by everyone. For example, if the intent and content of the message are not understood, the message has not been received, then the communication is considered to not be effective. It is not enough that you the <u>sender</u> knows what to say, it is the receiver who determines the meaning and understanding. Also, keep in mind that the media or medium that you use can either increase or limit understanding.

One way to help others understand your message, is by knowing and understanding completely the subject matter that you are communicating. Think about which media or medium is the best to convey your message, and say the version over and over to yourself, so that you can make it sound the best way possible, and in your own words. The emphasis and emotion that you apply to your communications, will determine their effectiveness.

Think about which media or medium is the best to convey your message.

How fast people respond to your communication is very important. Remember that without <u>feedback</u> there is no communication. We must keep in mind, that what feedback we receive is dependent on how well we communicated, and how well the message was understood, unfortunately it may not be what we wanted to hear.

We also need to consider how formal or informal the communication is. Remember that formal communication requires more precision and accuracy, than informal communication. Experts tell us that ideal communication is a balance of formal and informal communication. There are a few other pointers to good communication, for example, humor can be very stimulating and acceptable, if properly used. Keep in mind that humor
requires a lot of experience and practice.

How fast people respond to your communication is very important. Remember that without feedback there is no communication.

II. The Manager's Role in Communications

All work revolves around communication, thus managers have no choice other than to be effective communicators. Ask yourself, how could you as a district manager, fulfill your duties, if you did not communicate to others? How can you get things done through others, without someone knowing about it?

As a District Sales Manager/communicator, keep the following in mind:

- All activity results from communication
- The most effective outcomes are usually achieved as a result of effective communication
- Ineffective communications are very costly
- Direct communication, where others can see how you act and understand, are the most effective.

How you manage your communication, and your role is also very important, and you have to decide your role. Managers often see their role in organizations as <u>forwarders</u> of information who communicate it to their people. Some managers see their role as <u>filers</u> of information, and file it away some place, what is your role?

There are also managers who see themselves as messengers, who pass on information as they receive it, there are others who <u>massage</u> the information, before they pass it on, only you can be the judge of your role here.

A. Involve Others

One of the most important ways that a manager can be a good Communicator, is by involving others. We agree that communication requires transmitting messages to others. When you involve others, you need to make effort, and take the time. We will all agree that the best way to get this done, is to involve others. Involving others means a lot more than telling them what to do and delegating, it also requires talking and listening to them. When you don't involve others, you are telling them that you do not value their experiences and ideas.

All work revolves around communication, thus managers have no choice other then to be effective communicators.

Direct communication, where others can see how you act and understand, are the most effective.

One of the most important ways that a manager can be a good Communicator, is by involving others.

Remember that your success as a manager, depends on your sales people's success, get them involved in all communications.

Moreover, when you exclude others who have ideas to contribute, you are telling them what you really think about their contribution.

Remember that your success as a manager, depends on your sales people's success, get them involved in all communications.

III. Roadblocks to Good Communications

Some of the most common problems that we face with effective communications, are referred to as roadblocks. Now remember that <u>effective communication is communication that works.</u> Effective communication is achievable if we make the commitment, and your sales reps expect effective communications from you.

Effective communication can be considered precious, delicate and requires care.

Effective communication is considered like gold, it is very valuable and we do not receive it very often. Like gold, effective communication is a scarce and expensive resource. It also need s to go through a lot of refining before we receive it. Effective communication can be considered precious, delicate, and requires care.

Effective communication is measured by results, these results are usually informing or changing the behavior of others. It involves one person or a group, effectively receiving the message. How well people receive the message, depends on what "action" takes place as a result of the words. Remember, effective communication does not need to be complicated.

There are many roadblocks to communication that occur frequently, most of these roadblocks are because of you, others, or some things that are beyond your control.

Effective communication is measured by results, these results are usually informing or changing the behavior of others.

The roadblocks that take place are usually for a variety of reasons, either something that you do, or that others (the messengers or recipients) do, or there are some things that are third party influenced, and beyond your control.

A. You and Your Style

We all have our own particular communication style, and that style will be perceived by your audience in either a positive or negative way. One way that you can improve your communication style is by adapting it to the needs of your audience.

The planning and preparation that you do, greatly influences your style and effectiveness. Your motivations are very important in getting the message across.

The Six P's

Proper

Planning

Prevents

Particularly

Poor

Performance

When you prepare a presentation to others, there are a few cardinal rules to follow:

* Think about what you are going to say
* Know your audience as well as possible (Their knowledge level)
* Use a voice tone and volume that is appropriate
* Practice before the presentation

During the presentation, don't listen to yourself, let others tell you what they heard, and most of all watch your speed, all too often we speak too quickly.

Very often a common roadblock is our lack of clarity and consistency. The more <u>clear</u> we are about the message the better understood it will be. The more consistent that we are in our communication, the more trust and confidence we inspire in others.

Very often a common roadblock is our lack of clarity and consistency.

B. Credibility

You can't have trust and confidence when you lack credibility. We demonstrate credibility when we show that we are knowledgeable in a subject area. Others judge our credibility by how well we communicate our expertise. Credibility is important, but the only way to maintain it, is through honesty and truthfulness, distorting the truth can lessen your credibility.

C. Timing

As the old saying goes, "being in the right place at the right time is everything".

The receiver of the message plays a great role in how effective our communication is. Keep in mind that your audience, like you is very busy and constantly receiving messages from everyone. We need to determine the readiness level of the audience, the right time to deliver the message, the moment when it will be most effective. Sometimes we are in such a hurry to get our message out, that we use poor judgement on timing. As the old saying goes, "being in the right place at the right time is everything." Put yourself in the receiver's shoes, try to time your message to coincide with the receiver's needs and situation. Is now the right time? How long does the person have to listen to you?

With timing, there are a few important rules that we should observe, ask yourself these questions:

* Will the medium I use affect timing?
* Will the time I am allocated, affect what medium I use?
* When is the best time to communicate?
* Do you listen to your audience?
* Can <u>you</u> focus completely on this communication?
* Can the audience focus completely on this communication?
* Is everyone sure how long the message will be?
* Can you shorten the message and still be effective?

Your company's style can be a roadblock to effective communication. Things that determine the company's style are: its culture or personality the environment and the size of the company.

D. Your Company's Style

In every company there are characteristics that either inhibit of foster communication.

Your company's style can be a roadblock to effective communication. Things that determine the company's style are: its culture or personality, the environment and the size of the company.

Company's have their own individual styles of communication, and in every company there are characteristics that either inhibit or foster communication.

What is your company culture like? What is their style in managing?

* Participation
* Problems
* Decision Making
* Meetings
* Extent of Power and Control
* Rewards

What is your company's style as far as speed is concerned? Do people process communications quickly, are you expected to respond quickly, or is everything at slow pace?

The size of the company can influence communication greatly. In a large company you may find communication to be less personal, due to the size and levels of management. A small company is not always easy to communicate with either, in fact many times people in smaller companies have even less time to listen.

The environment of the company itself can greatly affect your communication. The physical layout can affect how you communicate. When people are in other areas, and other locations, this can greatly affect communications. These are mostly physical roadblocks, that you have no control over but you have to try to work around them in the best way possible.

E.   The Communications Process

The communications process can be a barrier depending on the method of communicating being used, the choice of media and the information being sent. Many times roadblocks occur due to:

* Communications Channels Used
* Information Overload
* Feedback
* Questions from Receivers

The communications channels that we use at times are not always the best for our audience. Personal Appearance, body language, tone and level of the speaker, can influence the effectiveness of our communications.

Currently information overload is one of the greatest problems that our audience faces.

Currently information overload is one of the greatest problems that our audience faces everyday. We need to be cognizant of this problem, and we need to try to focus all of our communications in a way that helps our audience deal with this wide variety of messages. This situation will not change, and with e-mails becoming more commonly used, the challenge to target our communications, is greater than ever.

Questions, are another roadblock to communication, people frequently ask questions, when they are not really seeking an answer. While questions can sometimes orientate us and set us back on the right track for good communications, more often they disrupt, delay, or cause problems.

A lack of response is another roadblock that frequently occurs.

A lack of response is another roadblock that frequently occurs. Often, we send a message and let the receiver decide what the message means. We may not control the reactions, feelings, and thoughts that the message may provoke. Often the type of media that we use, does not encourage a response, and even worse, many times we do not seek any kind of response at all.

The "rumor mill" is another roadblock to effective communication. Rumors exist in every company large and small, the best way to deal with them is by being aware of them, but most of all by being objective and focusing on your message. You cannot control rumors, and you should not let them inhibit your communication.

The "rumor mill" is another roadblock to effective communication

F. How to Overcome Communication Roadblocks

Follow these easy rules to overcome communication roadblocks:

1) Identify the causes of communication failures

2) Categorize the causes by – people, time, technology, and yourself

3) Put a plan together to improve communication, items to be considered are:

* Meeting with others involved in the communication process
* Look at better time management
* Look at your use of e-mail
* Look at your listening and presentation skills

4) Fix a date when you will review your plan , and stick to that date if possible

5) Make all communications as short and simple as possible

6) For important matters communicate in person

7) If you cannot be there, select a good messenger

8) Important communication should be more than one medium and be repetitive

IV. Effective Communication Techniques

The new communication channels are not making the manager's job any easier, all these options are a real challenge for the manager. Even though there is a lot of new communication technology, we can always improve our speech, writing, body language, as well as the media we decide to use. So our communications tools are basically the same, even though the technology has advanced.

Follow these rules to overcome roadblocks:

* **Identify the causes**

* **Categorize the causes**

* **Put a plan together to improve communication**

Important communication should be more than one medium and be repetitive.

We can always improve our speech, writing, body language, as well as the media we decide to use.

A. Verbal Communication

Try to communicate with less words when possible.

Speech is still the preferred choice of communication, but it is not without its problems. It is human nature to speak more than is necessary, but speaking less can often achieve more. Try to communicate with less words when possible. Less words are more effective, because it allows others to speak and gives you more time to listen. Use monosyllables more often, and use simple and plain words.

B. Written Communication

The best way to use written communication is simply, shortly and clear as possible.

Written communications still maintain a very important role in the business world. The best way to use written communication, is to get the message across as simply, shortly and clearly as possible. Follow these golden rules for written communications:

* Be organized, brief and concise
* Say it in as few words as possible
* Write with your target audience in mind (think of their needs)
* Realize that people will interpret your writing differently
* Make your writing impartial but understandable
* Try to generate a response and feedback

C. Visual Communication

When using visuals, graphics and color as much as possible.

Often in the workplace you will use visual aids such as charts, slides, graphics and overhead transparencies. When using visuals, use graphics and
color as much as possible. Color messages and graphics are a lot more powerful than type written words, and can help you to reach your audience more quickly and effectively. If you are using PowerPoint presentations, it is very easy to add in color and graphics. Use colors tastefully and appropriately, over use or poor color choice can diminish the impact of your presentation.

Over use or poor color choice can diminish the impact of your presentation.

D. Non Verbal Communication

Non verbal communication is another communication channel that is very important, in fact in many cultures it is even considered more important than what we say or write. Non verbal communication, (body language) Facial expressions and body movement, definitely reflect how we think and feel. In fact, experts say that 35% of communication is in body language. Things that we need to look for in non verbal communications are:

Experts say that 35% of communication is in body language.

* Eye contact, how we look at those whom we speak to
* Our appearance and how we dress when communicating
* How we behave in groups or with individuals
* Proximics, the amount of physical space and the distance we maintain from others

All of these non verbal communications activities can affect our communications.

Being able to respond quickly does not ensure the accuracy and understanding of our communication.

E. Office Technology

New office technology is the way of the future. These new tools help people to communicate more quickly and effectively. All of these tools help us to communicate faster, but the speed of being able to communicate quickly does not insure the quality of the communication. Being able to respond quickly does not ensure the accuracy and understanding of our communication. While we are on the subject of speed, remember that speaking too quickly can cause a problem. The speed of the communication should be according to the need of the receiver. New and speedy communications devices are no substitute for personal contact. Also the media that we decide to use can help or hinder the communication.

New and speedy communications devices are no substitute for personal contact.

V. What You Can Do To Be An Effective Communicator

Think through very carefully what you plan to communicate to your audience.

There are many things that you can do to be an excellent communicator. The most important thing that you can have as a communicator is self-confidence and project that self-confidence. Here are some good pointers about being an effective communicator. Always be aware that any communication can fail, you should always think through very carefully what you plan to communicate to your audience. Work on overcoming roadblocks that can affect your successful communication with others. Work at improving your listening habits, if you don't listen, intently you won't communicate effectively.

You need to work at getting the correct message across at all times.

There is a need to use different communication styles and methods when working with individuals or groups, as well as when communicating directly or indirectly with the audience. You need to work at getting the correct message across at all times, and you need to work at constantly improving your communication skills. Lastly, the timing of your communication has a definite impact on its effectiveness.

There is no substitute for face to face communication.

Communicating with individuals is very important, we need to give our attention to one to one communication, there is no substitute for face to face communication. We also need to involve others in the conversation, because recognition is communication. People like being heard and knowing that their opinion is respected. When we share our ideas with others, we build up relationships, and effective relationships increase communication effectiveness. When we persuade others to do something on our behalf, we are communicating. So as you can see, communicating with individuals and the human element is so important. Now we also need to look at communicating with groups.

Communicating with individuals and the human element is so important.

Communication with groups is also very important for a variety of reasons. Communication with groups, makes them into cohesive groups or teams. The group communication will serve to provide them with a purpose or sense of direction.

Standards and expectations are established through group communications. It has been found that group communications strengthen the groups as well as the individuals within the group. This communication helps you to make your district, into a more, cohesive, effective and motivated team.

Through communication with your district, you provide the support they need. By communicating with them, you provide clear direction and foster their productivity. Communication allows your district to achieve their goals, by providing them with the information and resources that they require to achieve their objectives. As a district manager, you can expect the reward and recognition for your success in resourcing and supporting projects and teams which report to you.

Communication with groups is also very important.

Group communications strengthen the groups as well as the individuals within the group.

Communication allows your district to achieve their goals.

Summary

Your major objective should be:

What do I want my 'audience' to do know or feel as a result of my communication?

The New Webster's Dictionary defines 'communications' as 'a system of facilities used for communicating messages or orders the combined study of effective communication in all forms including speech, writing, and graphic and dramatic arts.'

The importance of effective communication cannot be overstated. In order to communicate your communication effectively your major objective must answer the question:-

What do I want my 'audience' to do know or feel as a result of my communication?

> **Just because I've spoken doesn't mean I have been heard,**
> **Just because I've been heard doesn't mean I have been understood,**
> **Just because I've been understood doesn't mean I have been accepted,**
> **Just because I've been accepted doesn't necessarily mean there is going to be any change in behavior.**
>
> **Carl Jung**

Review Questions (Chapter VI)

DIRECTIONS. Circle the letter corresponding to the correct answer for each question.

1. For communication to be effective there are certain elements that should be considered **except:-**
   a. The subject matter (basic or advanced)
   b. Knowledge of the receiver
   c. The media that will deliver the communication
   d. Formal or informal presentation

2. Factors that need to be kept in mind **except:-**
   a. All activity results from communication
   b. The most effective outcomes are usually achieved as a result of effective communication
   c. Ineffective communications are very costly
   d. Direct communication, where others can see how you act and understand, are the most effective
   e. The communicator needs to be bi-lingual

3. Things that determine the company's style include **except:-**
   a. Its culture
   b. Its personality
   c. Its annual turnover
   d. Its environment

4. The following rules will help you to overcome communication roadblocks **except:-**
   a. Categorize the causes by people, time technology and yourself
   b. For important matters communicate in e-mail
   c. Examine your listening and presentation skills
   d. Look at better time management

Answers to Review Questions

1.   B

2.   E

3.   C

4.   B

VII. LEADERSHIP AND MOTIVATION

I. INTRODUCTION

As we now know from references in former chapters, the primary aim of a District Sales Manager is to increase the individual teams productivity and to contribute to the achievement of the company's goals and objectives. Motivation and leadership go hand in hand, effective leaders inspire motivation. Motivation is internal but is influenced by external forces eg. A professional leader in the shape of a District Sales Manager.

The District Sales Manager achieves these objectives through, not for, others. This achievement is gained through the leadership qualities of the District Sales Manager. A Manager may excel in planning, organizing, staffing, making decisions and controlling the operation but unless the team carries out the work planned the outcomes that are expected from them, will not be forthcoming.

Primary aim of a District Sales Manager is to increase the individual teams productivity.

What is a Leader?

A leader is described as a person who leads, guides, conducts, directs, influences and has the ability to motivate people toward achieving their goals willingly, displaying enthusiasm, tenacity and persistence.

The Question is often asked "Are Leader's Born or Made?"
One famous leader, politician when asked this question replied "I wasn't born a leader I was born a baby!" (Winston Churchill). He is acknowledged as one of the world's most famous leader's and motivator.

A leader is described as a person who leads, guides, conducts, directs, influences and has the ability to motivate people toward achieving their goals willingly.

Objectives

These learning objectives will help you focus your attention on learning outcomes after this section you should be able to:

1.   Describe the characteristics and requirements of a District Manager as a leader and motivator.
2.   Describe the five common leadership styles.
3.   Describe how a manager demonstrates concern for others and motivates them to raise their performance.

Key Concepts

1. As a leader, it is your role to obtain the results and outcomes required by senior management.

2. To meet the individual needs of each person in the team.

3. To ensure that your people perform as a team.

The characteristics and requirement of a District Sales Manager as a leader.

Plan to optimize the achievement of results, by setting and prioritizing personal and team objectives.

(1) The major characteristics of an effective leader are that you know yourself and understand your personality, strengths and weaknesses as a leader and are able to take the appropriate steps to self improvement.

(2) You plan to optimize the achievements of results, by setting and prioritizing personal and team objectives.

(3) You manage others to optimize results by:-
     (a) Showing sensitivity to the needs of others.
     (b) Obtaining the commitment of others.
     (c) Presenting positively to others.
     (d) Relating to others.

You manage yourself to optimize results by:-
* **Demonstrating self confidence and personal drive.**
* **Managing personal emotions and stress.**
* **Managing personal learning and development.**

(4) You manage yourself to optimize results by:-
     (a) Demonstrating self confidence and personal drive.
     (b) Managing personal emotions and stress.
     (c) Managing personal learning and development.

(5) You use your intellect to optimize results by:-
     (a) Collecting and distributing information.
     (b) Identifying and applying concepts.
     (c) Making decisions.

(6) Demonstrate concern for others by:-

    (a) Using change as an opportunity for improvements.

    (b) Establishing and communicating high expectations of performance.

    (c) Actively seeking to do things better.

    (d) Striving to identify and break down the barriers to excellence.

Demonstrate concern for others by:-

Actively seeking to do things better.

(7) You strive to know your Sales Representative better by:-

    (a) Demonstrating acceptance of others holding different views.

    (b) Making time available to help and support others when they are encountering difficulties.

    (c) Reinforcing their self worth and value in what they do during counseling sessions.

Making time available to help and support others.

(8) You encourage your team to:-

    (a) Express themselves honesty by actively seeking to identify and clarify their attitudes, views and feeling towards others.

(9) You demonstrate commitment by:-

    (a) Taking personal responsibilities for making things happen.

    (b) Confronting difficult issues openly.

    (c) Continually identifying and creating opportunities for new initiative.

You demonstrate commitment by:-
* Taking personal responsibilities for making things happen.

(10) You take on the responsibility for training and developing each member of the team by

    (a) Establishing learning and developing needs for the individual and team by completing a training needs analysis.

    (b) Identifying strengths and weaknesses in product knowledge, anatomy and physiology, communication and selling skills.

Establishing learning and developing needs for the individual and team.

(c)   Encouraging individuals and assisting them to evaluate their own learning and development needs and then setting specific, measurable attainable, relevant and learning objectives to optimize the use of the available resources.

The qualities of a District Sales Manager.

The qualities of a District Sales Manager that, if not inherent, need to be developed, as these are qualities that sales people expect.

1. Consistency

People today expect to know where they stand with their manager whether they posses a degree or not, whether they are experienced or inexperienced.

2. Competence

Is considered an authority on the subject and has the skills and knowledge to do anything that is expected of the Sales Representative.

3. Fairness

Demonstrates no favoritism to man or woman, young or old.

4. Honesty

Is upfront with praise and is sincere about it; when needing to be critical is not destructive but constructive.

5. Humane

Makes no exceptions treats everybody as human beings regardless of color, religion or sex.

6. Decisive

Tough and unpopular decisions will be made regardless of the fact that some feelings may be hurt.

7. Courageous

Doesn't tolerate mediocre performance and will terminate, if attitude is wrong and results are not achieved.

Consistency

Competence

Fairness

Honesty

Humane

Decisive

Courageous

8. Loyalty

Does not pass the buck takes responsibility when things go wrong.

9. Delegator

Knows who, where and when to delegate to obtain the optimum results required.

10. Sensitivity

Sensitive to the needs, problems and situations that occur within a sales team both business and personal.

11. Empathetic

Able to put yourself in the other persons shoes.

If you as a District Sales Manager expect to have exceptional management relationships with your team and each member of your team you may need to work on developing the necessary qualities if they are deficient in your personality profile.

C. Management Influence and Effectivity

How effective you are as a leader within your role as a District Sales Manager will be dependant on your ability to influence and in turn be influenced by the people in your team in achieving the many tasks that you will be given.

The way that a District Sales Manager exerts influence over the members of the sales team is by earning the respect of each Sales Representatives. You cannot demand respect you have to earn it. You earn respect by demonstrating the qualities that were referred to on previous pages in this section such as loyalty, sensitivity, empathy, humanity, courage, decisiveness. While you have the authority to get certain things carried out because of the title that the company has bestowed upon you it is 'Personal influence which will induce your people to achieve the goals and tasks set them enthusiastically and willingly and not influenced by authority, this way they do not feel obligated and act as through the decisions and ideas are their own.

Loyalty

Delegator

Sensitivity

Empathetic

How effective you are as a leader will be dependant on your ability to influence and in turn be influenced by the people in your team.

Increasing your Influence over the Team

* Most representatives consistently look to their manager for guidance, direction and advice. If and when this happens don't respond in an authoritarian manner. As this response may result in your team not approaching you in the future.

* Maintain their respect by keeping the communication channels open and uncomplicated. Keep them informed of all developments that concerns them, with both good and bad news.

It is critical for the manager to have the team co-operate willingly.

* It is critical for the manager to have the team co-operate willingly, the manager encourages this by:-

(a) Creating friendships, by letting them know you are sincere in your aims to help them and that you appreciate the job that they do and you will only be successful if they are successful.

(b) Help them help themselves by providing them with consistent and exceptional 'on the job training.'

Salespeople need consistent strong leadership to counteract the eroding elements of the job.

(c) Salespeople need consistent strong leadership to counteract the eroding elements of the job, cancelled appointments, two minute calls, 'will not see' healthcare professionals, exceptional weather conditions, non receptive gatekeepers etc. Managers must provide the kind of leadership that inspires confidence and competence.

Managers must provide the kind of leadership that inspires confidence and competence.

Leadership and Motivational Styles

Autocratic Dictatorship Style

Everything is black and white, top down communication. Feedback is not required orders are given to be carried out, not up for discussion this style assumes sales people are lazy not responsible for their actions.

Democratic – Participative Style

Management assumes that sales people are responsible and imaginative and ambitious.
The democratic – participative style of and ambitious.
Committee style of management however final decisions are usually made by managers after consultations if there are risks in the decisions.

Laissez – Faire Style

The manager does not tend to exert any authority on the group. This manager lets the group and individuals make up their own minds and interferes minimally.

Manipulative – Inspirational Style

This manager leads by controlling and playing one salesperson against another to produce better results. Very structured little or no team involvement in setting targets, goals etc.

Benevolent Autocracy Style

Management is usually decisive and authoritarian but actively seek participation in the decision making process. Management makes final decisions.
A saying reported to be from Winston Churchill regarding the democratic process stated that democracy was the worst kind of government until you considered the alternative (he was probably thinking at the time of Russia, the Japanese or German method of government—Dictatorship).

A saying reported to be from Winston Churchill regarding the democratic process stated that "Democracy was the worst kind of government, until you considered the alternative" (he was probably thinking at the time of the Russian, Japanese and German method of government – Dictatorship).

Summary

*   As a leader it is the District Sales Manager's responsibility to obtain the required results though, not for the team.

*   To plan, organize staff, make decisions manage interpersonal relationships and the individuals within the team so that:-

(a) Each person within the team feels that they are playing a vital part and contributing significantly in the success of the team

(b) The team acts and performs like a team.

How well you manage the individual relationships within your team will determine your success as a leader in your role as a District Sales Manager.

Management skills and leadership skills are not inherent they need to be learned, developed and practiced so that you can grow into becoming a better manager – remember the saying "amateurs practice until they get things right and stop – professionals practice until they never get things wrong"!

How well you manage the individual relationships within your team will determine your success as a leader in your role as a District Sales Manager.

LEADERSHIP AND MOTIVATION 137

Leadership – Checklist

A. Do you spend sufficient time in the field with sales reps?

Yes ☐   No ☐   Comments _____

B. Are these field contacts aligned to priorities?

Yes ☐   No ☐   Comments
_____

C. Are you satisfied that field contacts have good business purpose? Are tangible results in evidence?

Yes ☐   No ☐   Comments
_____

D. Are you fully capable to develop the knowledge and skills of sales reps?

Yes ☐   No ☐   Comments
_____

E. Do you have the skill to counsel sales reps effectively?

Yes ☐   No ☐   Comments
_____

F. Do you the sales reps under your responsibility have the necessary knowledge, skills and attitudes to achieve sales commitments? Are they highly proficient in the following:

1. Knowledge of territory? Key accounts?

Yes ☐ No ☐ Comments
_____

2. Knowledge of company policies and procedures?

Yes ☐ No ☐ Comments
_____

3. Product knowledge including benefits?

Yes ☐ No ☐ Comments
_____

4. Knowledge of pharmacology, medicine etc?

Yes ☐ No ☐ Comments
_____

5. Knowledge of sales principles and techniques?

Yes ☐ No ☐ Comments
_____

6. Knowledge of themselves, their strengths and weaknesses?

   Yes ☐   No ☐   Comments _____

7. Skill in planning and managing their territories?

   Yes ☐   No ☐   Comments _____

8. Skill in setting specific and measurable objectives for each sales call?

   Yes ☐   No ☐   Comments _____

9. Skill in establishing rapport?

   Yes ☐   No ☐   Comments _____

10. Skill in probing (questioning) techniques?

    Yes ☐   No ☐   Comments _____

11. Skill in opening a sales discussion?

    Yes ☐   No ☐   Comments _____

12. Skill in translating technical facts into physician/or patient benefits?

    Yes ☐   No ☐   Comments _____

13. Skill in using visual aids?

    Yes ☐   No ☐   Comments _____

14. Skill in dealing with physician feedback-handling objections (resistance)?

    Yes ☐   No ☐   Comments _____

15. Skill in closing the sale (obtaining commitments to prescribe)?

    Yes ☐   No ☐   Comments _____

16. Skill in solving problems?

    Yes ☐   No ☐   Comments _____

17. Skill in developing big business from target accounts?

    Yes ☐   No ☐   Comments _____

18. Skill in report writing and in sending meaningful feedback to the information center?

Yes ☐   No ☐   Comments _____

G. Do you have an efficient system for training new sales reps?

Yes ☐   No ☐   Comments _____

H. Are new reps adequately oriented to their new responsibilities?

Yes ☐   No ☐   Comments _____

I. In addition to new employees, is a program for continuous training and development in effect? Is this ongoing training based on periodic measurements of training needs?

Yes ☐   No ☐   Comments _____

J. Is sufficient training being given to the job-related activities of the reps?

Yes ☐   No ☐   Comments _____

K. Would you say you are proficient in the following areas:

1. Getting things done?

Yes ☐   No ☐   Comments _____

2. Meeting sales goals and objectives?

Yes ☐   No ☐   Comments _____

3. Directing and guiding those reporting to you?

Yes ☐   No ☐   Comments _____

4. Leading and motivating?

Yes ☐   No ☐   Comments _____

5. Using interpersonal skills?

Yes ☐   No ☐   Comments _____

6. Communicating with your people and management?

Yes ☐   No ☐   Comments _____

7. Being really innovative?

Yes ☐ No ☐ Comments _____

8. Solving problems?

Yes ☐ No ☐ Comments _____

9. Coping with administration and making the optimum use of management time?

Yes ☐ No ☐ Comments _____

L. When developing sales reps, are updated training methods and materials used?

Yes ☐   No ☐   Comments _____

M. Do you have a communication system in place whereby important information is promptly communicated?

Yes ☐   No ☐   Comments _____

N. Have you assured communications with each sales rep regarding:

1. Policy and procedures?

Yes ☐ No ☐ Comments _____

2. Updated job description?

Yes ☐ No ☐ Comments _____

3. Individual standards of performance?

Yes ☐ No ☐ Comments _____

O. Are cycle meetings productive?

Yes ☐   No ☐   Comments _____

P. Are there other criteria you deem important to measure-relative to your responsibility for building a high-caliber sales force?

Yes ☐   No ☐   Comments _____

Review Questions (Chapter VII)

DIRECTIONS. Circle the letter corresponding to the correct answer for each question.

1. A manager's leadership skills will be measured by:-
   a. Performance to the budget
   b. How well a manager manages the individual relationship within the team
   c. Increasing sales every year by 20%
   d. Reducing the turnover of staff

2. A manager demonstrates concern for others by:-
   a. Using change as an opportunity for improvements
   b. Establishing and communicating high expectations of performance
   c. Actively seeking to do things better
   d. All of the above

3. Demonstrating commitment includes the following except:-
   a. Taking personal responsibilities for making things happen
   b. Selling to difficult customers that the representative can't handle
   c. Continually identify and create opportunities for new initiative
   d. Confronting difficult issues openly.

4. You take on the responsibility for training and developing each member of the team by
   a. Establishing learning and developing needs for the team by completing a training needs analysis.
   b. Identifying individual strengths and weaknesses in product knowledge, anatomy and physiology, communication and selling skills
   c. Studying weekly reports and telling representatives what they should do
   d. Analyzing marketing and sales reports and then telling the team what they should do

Answers to Review Questions

1.   B

2.   D

3.   B

4.   B

VIII. CONTROLLING

I. THE CONTROL FUNCTION

Management is planning, organizing, leading and controlling the activities of others in the same organization in order to attain or exceed desired objectives. The basic purpose of planning is to ensure that company objectives are reached as rapidly and efficiently as possible. Then all resources must be organized in such a way as to carry out these plans as rapidly and efficiently as possible. The manager must direct or lead the activities of the people who make up the organization, to carry out those plans as rapidly and efficiently as possible. Finally all of the functions must be examined at frequent intervals to ensure that everything is going according to plan. This is the control function, which includes the performance appraisal or evaluation of those people reporting to the manager. (Refer further to Chapter IX).

All of the functions must be examined at frequent intervals to ensure that everything is going according to plan. This is the control function.

Objectives

These learning objectives will help you focus your attention on learning outcomes. After completing this section you should be able to:

1. Describe the purpose of the control function.
2. List the steps to be taken to ensure the control function is carried out effectively.
3. Describe the aspects of each representatives work that should be evaluated.

It is necessary to control results but this needs to be linked with controlling performance.

Key Concepts

1. Planning, organizing, leading and controlling activities of others is critical to a District Sales Manager being successful.
2. It is necessary to control results but this needs to be linked with controlling performance.

A. MANAGING CONTROL FUNCTIONS

In addition to ensuring that the sales representatives work according to plan and reach their objectives, the control function also has the following purposes:

* To ensure that representatives follow company policy and procedures while working;

* To identify problems and dangers before they can do any harm; and

* To take corrective action on time, if necessary

In doing so, we not only control, but further support important job activities. Controlling leads to the following alternatives:

1) Taking no action if it is seen that the original plan is being carried out correctly, and the objectives are being met.

2) Correcting actions if the original plan is deemed adequate, but is not being carried out properly.

3) Modifying the action plan if it is seen that it is not as realistic or effective as originally thought.

4) Modifying the objectives themselves if it turns out that they are not attainable or attractive after all.

To be useful, the control function must be:

Timely. Untimely action does not help correct problems or deviations in time to meet budget.

Accurate. Inaccurate information can do more harm than good, leading one to modify things that are all right, to cover or under react, or to ignore things that need correcting.

Economical. The whole process of gathering and analyzing information, making decisions, and taking action must be less expensive than the benefits it brings or the problems it is meant to correct.

Practical. The process must be as simple and quick as possible to carry out. Otherwise it could be abandoned, though people might continue to pay lip service to it.

Prioritized. Since not everything can be controlled at once, priorities must be set to ensure that the most important things get adequate attention.

The control function also has the following:-

To ensure that representatives follow company policy and procedures.

To identify problems and dangers

To take corrective action on time, if necessary

To be useful, the control function must be:

Timely

Accurate

Economical

Practical

Prioritized

B. EVALUATING THE CONTROL FUNCTION

To carry out the control function effectively, the District Manager must be able to:-

*   Measure the extent to which objectives are being met,

*   Evaluate how effectively the action plans are being carried out, and

*   Decide whether the objectives or plans continue to be viable under changing conditions.

More specifically, the following aspects of each representative's work should be evaluated:

Controlling results alone is not sufficient, because:

Results	Performance
Sales vs. quota - by total line - by product being promoted - by type of client Market share vs. plan Expenses vs. budget Sales productivity	Selling skills Product knowledge Physician selection Detailing frequency Client service Implementation of company plans

Results at the present time could be satisfactory, but the quality and/or quantity of the work being done could gradually get worse. If these are not observed and corrected on time, future results will inevitably deteriorate.

If current results are not satisfactory, it is necessary to evaluate the quality and quantity of the work being done in order to be able to find and correct the causes of the trouble.

C. CONTROL TECHNIQUE

The following steps will help the District Manager carry out the control function more effectively.

1)   Periodically review everyone's objectives and action plans in order to have them prominent. It is very easy to forget or lose sight of them in the day-to-day activities in the field.

The District Manager must be able to:-

Measure the extent to which objectives are being met

Evaluate how effectively the action plans are being carried out

Decide whether the objectives continue to be viable under changing conditions

Controlling results alone is not sufficient

Periodically review everyone's objectives and action plans in order to have them prominent.

2) Establish a schedule of progress reviews for each objective and/or action. For example, check sales progress towards the cycle's quota in each territory on a weekly basis. Evaluate each sales representative's selling skills once a cycle.

3) Carry out each review on schedule

4) Analyze progress to determine any significant differences between objectives or planned actions and their results to date.

5) Find ways of correcting deviations and shortcomings.

6) Implement these corrective measures as quickly and appropriately as possible.

D. ACTIVITIES AND REPORTS

The District Manager begins controlling the work of his/her representatives by carefully studying their reports, then discussing those reports with them in order to:

- clarify discrepancies;
- understand the reasons for particular situations;
- give suggestions and offer help; and
- prove that the reports are useful and valuable, and not merely a formality.

Then the District Manager should go out into the field for personal observation of the situation. This is necessary for several reasons:

- Conditions in the field change rapidly. If the District Manager does not go there frequently, he or she will lose contact with current issues.
- The situation as described by the sales representatives in their reports might be inaccurate or incomplete. Effective corrective action cannot be taken on the basis of reports alone.
- The representative might not perceive or report certain things at all, though they may represent a potential threat or danger.
- To win the representative's respect and to get them to follow advice and instructions willingly and enthusiastically, district managers must prove that they have extensive field experience and practical knowledge. This can be done only through regular field visits.

The District Manager begins by carefully studying their reports in order:

Clarify discrepancies

Understand the reasons for particular situations

Give suggestions

Prove that the reports are useful and valuable

The District Manager should go out into the field for personal observation of the situation.

The District Manager should approach the field visit in two different ways;

1)   Accompany representatives on their routes, to observe their sales call techniques.

2)   Work a small personal territory to maintain a feel for all aspects of a representative's work. In doing so, he/she can guide representatives by example and personal experience.

Some representatives often resist, or at least dislike, having their district manager accompany them on sales calls, managers will help overcome this resistance and dislike by doing the following:-

- Convincing the sales representatives that these visits are not an expression of lack of trust or suspicion, but a way of helping them;

- Carrying out these visits regularly, equitably, and openly;

- Holding helpful, objective, and honest debriefing sessions with the representatives after all visits, in which positive reinforcement receives equal or more praise than criticism; and

- Selling the concept of self-control, whereby each representative is encouraged to analyze the reasons and find and implement his or her own solutions to any difficulties.

In this way the sales representative can gradually be conditioned to view follow-up visits on the part of the manager as beneficial, instead of unwelcome intrusion.

The fundamental purpose is to take corrective measures whenever any significant deviations from the original objectives or action plan are observed.

At any level within the organization there are some corrective measures that can be decided and implemented directly, without the necessity of getting authorization from above.

The District Manager should approach the field visit in two difference ways.

Sales representative can gradually be conditioned to view follow-up visits as beneficial

The fundamental purpose is to take corrective measures whenever any significant deviations from the original objectives or action plan are observed.

The object of any control system used in selling is to monitor and take appropriate action when unacceptable variances occur.

E. DISTRICT MANAGEMENT REPORTS

The District Manager should regularly report on the following:-

1) Progress made towards reaching significant objectives and implementing important actions plans;

2) Reasons for significant deviations; and

3) Actions taken, and results obtained, for all measures that fall within the district manager's direct decision making authority.

(Insert examples of field visit and progress reports here)

SUMMARY

The object of any control system used in selling is to monitor an individual's and team's performance against the marketing plan that has been set and take appropriate action when unacceptable variances occur. It is a valuable waste of time and money in setting targets of achievement and having a plan of action unless there is a method of evaluating the procedures.

Managers have to ensure that they devote their time to the parts of the business which are not running according to plan.

The basic problem for District Managers is that they are often working with a limited amount of time, money and other resources. Managers have to ensure that they devote their time to the parts of the business which are not running according to plan. As stated in the text to be effective the control system must be timely, accurate, economical, practical and prioritized.

Review Questions (Chapter VIII)

DIRECTIONS. Circle the letter corresponding to the correct answer for each question.

1. The control function has the following purpose(s):
    a. Ensure the representatives follow company policies and procedures
    b. Identify problems and dangers before they can evolve
    c. Take corrective action on time
    d. All of the above

2. To carry out the control function effectively, the District Manager must be able to:
    a. Measure the extent to which objectives are being met
    b. Evaluate how effectively action plans are being carried out
    c. Decide whether the objectives are viable under changing conditions
    d. All of the above

3. Controlling results alone is not sufficient because results at the present time could be satisfactory, but the quality and/or quality of the work being done could gradually get worse.
    a. True
    b. False

4. Which of the following steps help the District Manager carry out the control function effectively.
    a. Periodic review of objectives and action plans
    b. Scheduling progress reviews
    c. Finding ways of correcting deviations and short comings
    d. Telephoning sales representatives daily

5. Which is not a reason why a District Manager would discuss an activity report with a representative.
    a. To clarify discrepancies
    b. To understand reasons for particular situations
    c. Because management likes District Managers to discuss the reports
    d. To give suggestions and offer help

Answers to Review Questions

1.   D

2.   D

3.   A

4.   A, B, C

5.   C

IX. PERFORMANCE APPRAISAL

I. INTRODUCTION

The major aim of completing performance appraisals is to improve the performance of your sales team. By providing individual objective feedback on how they are performing overall and identifying areas of their work that require improvement. Appraisals are designed to motivate people not destroy them, the emphasis should be to build on their strengths as well as to overcome weaknesses.

The major aim of completing performance appraisals is to improve the performance of your sales team.

Objectives

The following objectives are provided to identify expected learning outcomes when you finish this section you should be able to:-

1. Describe the major sources of information for appraising a Sales Representative's performance.
2. Describe the five steps to planning and conducting an effective performance appraisal.

Key Concepts

1. A District Sales Manager needs to do whatever is necessary to improve the individual representatives performance.
2. You cannot manage people effectively unless you assess what they are doing and how they are doing it.
3. Sales Representative's perform better and more consistently when they know that their performance is being reviewed and measured.
4. Clear territory objectives and standards of performance provide the guidelines that a representative must have, to achieve what is expected.

There has never been a monument erected to an unsuccessful person.

A. Elements of an Appraisal System

To appraise people properly you need to know what you are appraising and convey the knowledge to your salespeople.

A properly conducted and productive performance appraisal motivates a Sales Representative to improve performance.

A properly conducted and productive performance appraisal motivates a Sales Representative to improve performance. Performance appraisals make the job more interesting and challenging. They improve skills and increase the chances for a successful sales career and they motivate enthusiasm.

A performance appraisal also identifies progress towards assigned goals. The appraisal system measures progress and provides feedback on strengths and weaknesses. A performance appraisal session reinforces desired skills and helps to maintain improved performance and intensity.

A performance appraisal opens lines of communication.

Another benefit is that it enhances communication. Sales representatives sell more effectively when they know what is expected   of them and what their sales goals are.

A performance appraisal opens lines of communication, so that both positive and negative feelings can be expressed and a better understanding established.

Step I   Establish Performance Standards

Establish performance standards.

Establishing specific standards against which to measure performance. People perform better when they know that their performance is being measured and when they know what is expected of them. So the first step is to make sure you have standards, and when you do, you need to periodically review and update them.

Step II   Measure the Performance

Measure the performance.

A good performance appraisal measures total performance, product knowledge, selling skills, territory management, sales target achievement; make sure that you allocate the appropriate time to complete this step.

Step III   Plan the Appraisal

Planning the appraisal. This is vital – it also takes time. It is not a pleasant task to tell someone that he/she is not performing well in specific areas. This requires proper planning to do it right. Similarly the strengths need reinforcing and you must also plan for this. If you anticipate all of the potential problems before the interview, it will significantly reduce the risk of things getting out of hand.

Proper

Planning

Prevents

Particularly

Poor

Performance

Step IV   Conduct the Appraisal

There are many techniques involved in conducting the interview. The next step depends on your knowledge and skill in handling the performance discussion and the questions, concerns and problems that can surface. It is important that you get the sales representative involved – and that also takes skill.

Step V   Formulate a Specific Plan

Finally, the outcome of your performance appraisal should be a specific plan, based on your observations and discussions; even the good performers need your help in establishing and maintaining development plans (both short and long term).

If you are to have an effective performance appraisal system, you need to establish specific, measurable and realistic standards.

If you are to have an effective performance appraisal system, you need to establish specific, measurable and realistic standards. The best place to start with in relation to setting standards is the job description because this provides you with a list of duties and responsibilities (refer to Job Description and Performance of Standards).

You probably already have these in your own company but it may be of value for you in reviewing and updating yours, if required. The major sources of information for appraising a sales representative's performance are as follows:

*   Job Description
*   Performance Standards
*   Review of daily/weekly reports
*   Review of territory program and territory analysis
*   Sales statistics and target achievement
*   Exercise reports
*   Itineraries, versus calls achieved
*   Previous performance appraisals
*   Review of promotion cycle results
*   Correspondence
*   Critical incident file

B. Factors that Effect the Appraisal

Once you have all of the above you are now in a sound position to prepare for the appraisal interview. You should consider the following suggestions for conducting the actual meeting.

*   Allow time for meetings and give advance notice to the Sales Representative
*   Arrange for total privacy, free of interruptions
*   Establish your major objective
*   Plan to set the stage – create the right environment
*   Identify major strengths and where performance needs to be improved.
*   Anticipate resistance
*   Design a development plan

The characteristic of a good performance standard is that it should be <u>realistic</u>, so that it can be achieved.

The characteristic of a good performance standard is that it should be <u>realistic,</u> so that it can be achieved. If the bar is too high, the high jumper will get frustrated and quit. A good standard should always be within reach, require some stretch, but be achievable.

Now let's practice developing <u>specific</u>, <u>measurable</u> and <u>realistic</u> standards. The best place to start is with a Job Description or list of duties and responsibilities. Ideally, there should be one or more standards for every responsibility.

We have provided a model Job Description for a typical Sales Representative. It contains major responsibilities. Keep in mind the fact that Job Responsibilities may vary from company to company. For example, responsibility (sales achievement) may not be feasible to evaluate in your market as sales are pooled and individual sales achievements are impossible to determine.

C.   Performance Standards

We would like you to develop one or more standards for each responsibility. Try, where possible, to develop standards of a type which you as the District Manager actually will be able to observe and measure during fieldwork in your district. In other words, be realistic.

Read the list of responsibilities (refer to your current Job Description) then turn to the exercise on page 163 where you will be asked to develop observable and measurable standards.

You will recall that the second step in performance appraisal is appraising the total performance against these standards. This is relatively easy to do when you have good standards and are willing to make an ongoing and complete analysis of each Sales Representative's performance. You can then simply compare the standards with the performance. Collecting performance data is a must and should be a constant process. To successfully accomplish the task, however, you should maintain what is called a "critical incident" file. In this file you collect notes, data, or correspondence on major problems or successes for each representative. At appraisal time, you use your critical incident file and in addition, record every piece of data and information relating to performance – reports, observations, and so on. Obviously, there's no real limit to the amount of information on performance that you might have, but it is important that you have access to it at this time to truly measure the performance of each individual. This may surprise you, but you will find that you probably have specific sources of information available to use in the appraisal process.

Develop standards of a type which you as the District Manager will be able to observe and measure during fieldwork.

Collecting performance data is a must and should be a constant process.

It's important that you have some framework for organizing, measuring and rating their performance, item by item.

Once you have sufficient, and hopefully, complete data on a salesperson, it's important that you have some framework for organizing, measuring and rating their performance, item by item. If you do not have a performance appraisal form, you can use the one we have provided on page 163. Take a few minutes to study this.

After reviewing the performance appraisal you should be ready to use it applying some of the principles we have discussed. Your assignment now is to complete an appraisal on one of the Sales Representative's in your team.

Review each of the performance standards and rate their overall performance.

Review each of the performance standards and rate their overall performance. On the righthand side are three levels of performance: <u>Below</u> standard, <u>meets</u> standard, <u>exceeds</u> standard. First read your rep's case history. Then fill in the appropriate information where possible, and based on your analysis, rate their overall performance for each of the seven major areas.

## D.	Planning the Appraisal Interview

Key Points

* You need to spend the appropriate amount of time on planning and the Sales Representative must also have time to think about the forthcoming appraisal interview.

* Companies usually carry out an annual or six monthly performance appraisal on their salespeople. As this is an important occasion for both the District Sales Manager and the Sales Representative. This should be reflected in the quality of the planning that goes into it.

You need to spend the appropriate amount of time on planning the forthcoming appraisal interview.

* You will need to give each Sales Representative one to two weeks notice regarding their appraisals this should not come as a surprise. A good practice to get into, is to provide the Sales Representatives with a blank performance appraisal form and have them do a self-appraisal prior to the review meeting. This technique motivates the Sales Representatives to analyze their own performance.

They often discover some of their own weaknesses and this makes your job easier. A common framework such as this enables you both to communicate more effectively and to negotiate any differences.

It is critical to have absolute privacy and not to be disturbed.

The next point is critical: arrange for absolute privacy, free of interruptions. If you decide to meet in the office, arrange ahead of time to not be disturbed, and close the door (s) when the meeting begins.

Performance appraisal is a very important and personal activity, devoted to exploring performance, concerns, attitudes and development. Most of what you discuss is private. Give it the dignity that it deserves and find a quiet, secluded and comfortable site for the meeting.

Performance appraisal is a very important and personal activity.

As part of your planning for this session you should establish a major objective that is specific, measurable and realistic. Ask yourself: "What do I want this Sales Representative to do differently after this session?" While your basic goal is to review and discuss total performance, your major objective should be aimed at identifying a major performance area. The objectives for each representative will be more focused – they will be specific, measurable, and relevant as they are based on comprehensive analysis and planning.

Give it the dignity that it deserves and find a quiet, secluded and comfortable site for the meeting.

II. Rehearse the Interview

In your planning you have to set the stage and get the Sales Representative to relax. Plan a suitable lead-in to establish a positive atmosphere and to define what you hope to accomplish. For example, here's one way you might start the meeting:- Commence by using the Representative's name John/Mary.

"This is a very important opportunity for both of us. During our meeting I would like to review and discuss your total performance, agree on the major issues, and together with you formulate some plans for your growth and development within the company."

In your planning you have to set the stage and get the Sales Representative to relax.

A.   Identify the Major Areas

This step in your planning is to identify the major areas – both strengths and weaknesses – for discussion. While you should review total performance in this session, it is much more effective if you review most performance areas in brief and concentrate on the really important skills. Look to identify one or two things the Sales Representative does best and reinforce them, and then identify the weakest areas for discussion, you will be able to concentrate on a limited number of items and cover them in depth. It will also help retention, so that you can leave the session with only a few points to remember and on which to focus.

One of the difficulties in performance appraisal is getting your Sales Representatives to understand and accept weaknesses.

1.   One of the difficulties in performance appraisal is getting your Sales Representatives to understand and accept their weaknesses. Planning will help overcome this situation. Knowing your Sales Representatives and anticipating their reactions will help, but planning will also contribute. Rather than confront Sales Representatives directly, you can plan questions and lead them to analyze and discover their own shortcomings. Try using a questions like this:-

"John/Mary – If we could turn the clock back! What are some of the things that you could have done differently or better to achieve your quota for the new OTC Antacid?"

When you do anticipate some disagreement or potential resistance, the best way to offset this is to have, documentation available.

2.   You should also anticipate some resistance. That's our next suggestion for planning. When you do anticipate some disagreement or potential resistance, the best way to offset this is to have, documentation available. A good response is helpful, and you can plan that too, but it's a good idea to document your comments and reinforce them. All the information you use when doing the appraisal should be on hand to support those quantitative areas where you expect resistance. Also, in the qualitative measurement areas, such as selling skills, be prepared to cite specific examples. Here is one example:

In the qualitative measurement areas, such as selling skills, be prepared to cite specific examples.

"John/Mary – You recall a few weeks ago when you were calling on Dr Jones, I made a specific point afterwards of noting that you were not following the selling strategy. You also wandered from the selling strategy on subsequent calls. Maybe that is a clue to why there is very little movement of this product in the pharmacies. What do you think?"

B.   Rehearse your Interview Approach

Finally, you should try to do some preliminary planning on strategies or actions that will help achieve your development objective for the Sales Representative.

However, do this action planning "in rough" since the ideal plan should be developed by the Sales Representative, or together with you during the performance appraisal session.

Now that we have discussed these points, we'd like you to plan a performance appraisal interview with one or your representative's. Use the Appraisal Interview Planner on page 163 to plan this segment of your Appraisal. It should follow the parts we have just discussed.

III. Conducting the Interview

If you have done your planning properly, this can be a relatively easy step However, you should be aware of some important do's and don'ts.

A. 1. Avoid discussions of personality. Discuss results and performance, which are the things you can change and improve.   Personality or personal traits – such as smiling, being aggressive, becoming more likeable – are difficult to define and to change. People will become very defensive when personal traits are introduced, so avoid this distraction.

You should try to do some preliminary planning on strategies or actions that will help achieve your development objective for the Sales Representative.

Avoid discussions of personality. Discuss results and performance, which are the things you can change and improve.

Make sure you reinforce good results, and that you do it consistently.

2. Make sure you reinforce good results, and that you do it consistently.

You should spend as much time on positive items as you do on trying to upgrade weak areas.

3. It is a good idea to encourage self-appraisal. As suggested earlier, one way to do this is to have each Sales Representative do a self-appraisal prior to the interview. But even if you do not use this option, at appropriate points during the interview have them review their own performance. This, of course, induces them to analyze reasons why they are doing certain things, and is much more effective than having you do the "telling". You can ask good leading questions such as "There are a number of occasions where I have observed your using sales aids incorrectly, or not at all. Why is this happening? Do you feel uncomfortable with sales aids?

Ii is a good idea to encourage self-appraisal.

4. Don't spend so much time on appraising negative or weak performance areas that you never get to planning for change. Make your point, try to get agreement, and then move quickly to plans for improving that specific skill or area. The benefit is in improvement.

Allow adequate time for discussion.

5. Allow adequate time for discussion. How much time is enough? This is difficult to answer because every situation is different. The <u>minimum</u> time would be one hour, but two or three hours may be needed. The important thing is to take as much time as you need to do the performance appraisal <u>properly</u>. Remember, this is a once, or twice a year activity – an important one for both you and the Sales Representative – so be prepared to stay as long as you need to accomplish your objectives and hear what the representative has to say.

Avoid discussions of compensation.

6. Avoid discussions of compensation. While performance obviously influences compensation, most experts agree that the two topics should be kept apart.

PERFORMANCE APPRAISAL 161

B. Performance Appraisal Guidelines

1. Discuss performance and results, do not get into disagreement about personalities. Discuss the good results that have been obtained and try to spend equal time on the good results as well as the areas that need improvement.

2. Encourage the representative to appraise him/herself, ask open questions to let each person analyze the recent results and what the individuals feel are their developmental needs. Stress that results can be improved. Do not dwell too long on areas needing improvement.

3. Do not hurry the interview, allow sufficient time, avoid discussion of changes in compensation and finally agree on an action plan for improvement.

4. If you practice the guidelines suggested, your performance appraisals will be more effective, more professional and most important, will play a significant role in the development of your sales representatives and motivate them towards improved performance.

Discuss performance and results, do not get into disagreement about personalities.

Encourage the representative to appraise him/ herself.

If your practice the guidelines suggested, your performance appraisals will be more effective, more professional and most important, motivate them towards improved performance.

5.	Establish a Specific Training Program
4.	Conduct the Appraisal Interview
3.	Plan the Appraisal Interview
2.	Appraise Total Performance Against Standards
1.	Establish Performance Standards

Steps in Performance Appraisal

C. Source of Information for Appraising a Sales Representative's Performance

Below you will find a list of the typical information that can and should be used to evaluate performance.

Thomas Edison was once asked "Why do you persist in trying to invent this thing called an electric light when you have failed 1000 times." At this Edison replied " I haven't failed 1000 times, I have found 1000 ways it doesn't work"! Just after that the electric light was born!

SOURCES OF INFORMATION

1.	Job description
2.	Performance standards
3.	Review of daily/weekly reports
4.	Review of the overall territory program and marketing results
5.	Sales statistics and target achievement
6	Territorial product sales analysis
7.	Expense reports
8.	Itineraries versus calls made
9.	Previous performance appraisal reports
10.	Review of promotion cycle results
11.	Correspondence
12.	Coaching notes
13.	Critical incident file

D. PERFORMANCE STANDARDS

Sales Representative:………………………….. Date:………………..

Territory:…………………………………… **RATING**

	Below	Meets	Exceeds

A. Sales Achievements
1. Actual vs Goal ☐ ☐ ☐
2. Product Balance (Mature Products) ☐ ☐ ☐
3. New Product Growth ☐ ☐ ☐
NOTES: -
- -

B. Physician Calls
1. Number of Visits vs Plan ☐ ☐ ☐
2. VIP Coverage ☐ ☐ ☐
3. Physician Profile ☐ ☐ ☐
4. Physician Relationship ☐ ☐ ☐
5. Setting Objectives ☐ ☐ ☐
6. Quality of calls/selling skills ☐ ☐ ☐
NOTES: -
- -

C. Sales Outlets
1. Number of Visits vs Plan ☐ ☐ ☐
2. Servicing Inventory and Ordering ☐ ☐ ☐
3. Development of O.T.C Sales ☐ ☐ ☐
4. Keeping Pharmacists Informed ☐ ☐ ☐
NOTES: -
- -

D. Institutions
1. Number of Visits vs Plan ☐ ☐ ☐
2. Quality of Personal Contacts ☐ ☐ ☐
3. Awareness of Stock Position ☐ ☐ ☐
4. Products on Formulary ☐ ☐ ☐
NOTES: -
- -

E. Knowledge & Self Development
1. Responsiveness to Field Work & Coaching ☐ ☐ ☐
2. Ability to Answer Customer Questions ☐ ☐ ☐
3. Cycle Meeting Participation ☐ ☐ ☐
4. Knowledge of Competition ☐ ☐ ☐
5. Knowledge of Disease States ☐ ☐ ☐
6. CME Completion ☐ ☐ ☐
NOTES: -
- -

'If at first you don't succeed don't worry you are batting about even.'

Source Unknown

Summary

The review of a person's performance is a very valuable mechanism for motivating them toward improving their knowledge, skills, attitude and self worth, and in turn successful outcomes.

A performance appraisal focuses on two areas. The District Sales Manager's ability to:

(A)   Appraise and identify the areas of performance that need to be ad dressed.

(B)   The competence and confidence to be able to communicate this effectively to each Sales Representative.

It is essential to establish performance standards so the each Sales Representative clearly understands the job requirements and what is expected of them in the workplace.

Personal appraisal is the single most important form of task relevant feedback a District Sales Manager can provide a Sales Representative.

Personal appraisal is the single most important form of task relevant feedback a District Sales Manager can provide a Sales Representative.

Review Questions (Chapter IX)

DIRECTIONS. Circle the letter corresponding to the correct answer for each question.

1. The best place to start in relation to setting standards is to:-
   a. Review daily, weekly reports
   b. Review territory program
   c. Review itinerary versus calls achieved
   d. Review job description

2. Performance standards should be:-
   a. Relevant, realistic, specific
   b. Measurable, specific, realistic
   c. Specific, measurable, personal
   d. Measurable, relevant, specific

3. A properly conducted and productive appraisal includes the following **except**:-
   a. Helps a representative get promoted
   b. Identifies progress towards assigned goals
   c. Motivates a representative to improve performance
   d. Enhances communications

4. Elements of an appraisal system includes all of the following **except**:-
   a. Establishing performance standards
   b. Measuring performance
   c. Planning the appraisal
   d. Conducting the appraisal
   e. Reviewing salary for next year

5. Sources of information for appraising performance consist of the following **except**:-
   a. Job description, performance standards
   b. Reports review, territory results
   c. Sales statistics and target achievement
   d. Dinner meetings held

Answers to Review Questions

1.   A

2.   B

3.   A

4.   E

5.   D

X. TRAINING NEW REPRESENTATIVES

I. Pre-Class Training

Wile the company sales training department has the responsibility for:-

(A)   Overall planning, scheduling and coordination of the initial class training of new Sales Representatives.

(B)   Conducting the in-house training sessions of the class training.

It is the District Sales Manager's responsibility to see that each new Sales Representative is fully prepared for this formal training.   This can be achieved by implementing a pre-class training program through the utilization of a self-directed learning system designed specifically for pharmaceutical selling, (refer pages 170 – 171).

Objectives

These learning objectives will help you focus your attention on learning outcomes.   After completing this section you should be able to:-

1.   Describe the elements of an effective induction system.
2.   List the 'topics for discussion' during the induction process.
3.   Discuss the two primary considerations regarding technical training program developments.
4.   Describe the basic personality types and how to deal with them.

Key Concepts

1.   The District Sales Manager is the cornerstone to completing effective new representative inductions.
2.   How quickly a new representative settles in is dependant on the District Sales Manager ensuring that the induction process is carried out effectively and efficiently.

This section will comprise of three elements.

1.   Pre-Class Training
2.   Class Training
3.   Coaching – (Post Class Training)

It is the District Sales Manager's responsibility to see that each new Sales Representative is fully prepared for this formal training.

Recommended text 'Pharmaceutical Selling in a Changing Environment – T.B.Yeats Newwave Selling - V.F Peters

A. New Representative Orientation

It is crucial for the 'new person' to be welcomed to the company the right and professional way. This should be in the form of a letter congratulating the new person on being selected from an exceptional group of applicants. This 'welcome' letter should refer to the fact that the manager, team and company are pleased to have the new hire join their 'District Sales Force'. The initial letter should also contain information regarding:-

* Company policies and procedures
* Compensation
* Conditions of work
* The job description – nominated territory

* Confirmation of the day, time, place and person to report to on the first day of orientation.
* A training and development guide covering the induction course should also be included in the greeting package with selected anatomy physiology/product learning systems for pre-study.

It is the industry's experience that new sales people who are appropriately inducted into a pharmaceutical company and know exactly what is expected of them, tend to adapt more quickly, perform more effectively and stay longer.

It is also the manager's responsibility to ensure that the materials needed to do the job are ordered/provided e.g.

* All training materials/hardware
* Business cards
* Territory records (electronic/hard copy)
* Learning systems anatomy physiology product manuals, etc.

A letter should be sent to <u>all the staff</u> in the home office introducing the new hire, providing some background information, territory to be worked and the date of commencement.

New sales people who are appropriately inducted into a pharmaceutical company and know exactly what is expected of them. Tend to adapt more quickly, perform more effectively and stay longer.

B. Transition Period – The First Day

Your objectives should be on the first day to ensure that:

1. The transition from the new hire to a team member is as pleasant as possible.

2. All the necessary company requirements are known to the inductee; e.g.

   A. Reports, expenses etc.

   B. Formal and informal practices

   C. Company employment information that needs to be completed.

   D. A place for the rep has been allocated for his/her use office/ desk/phone etc.

   E. Storage of promotional materials

   F. Contact people, phone/fax numbers, mobiles, e-mail, etc.

   G. The Representative is provided with all necessary materials that will be needed for the induction period.

   H. The representative knows or has information about car policy, accidents, hiring, breakdowns, etc.

The transition from the new hire to a team member is as pleasant as possible.

C. Pre Work Training and Education

A vital part of a District Sales Manager's responsibility is to ensure that during the pre-class phase of a New Representative's induction period, they are provided with product and educational materials to be studied and understood prior to attending head office for their official training period; this can be adequately taken care of by utilizing a program that is designed specifically for pre-class training, supported by company literature, reprints etc.

Utilizing a program that is designed specifically for pre-class training, supported by company literature, reprints etc.

D. Training Program Development

**Two primary considerations.
1. The specific information that must be communicated.
2. How that information is to be presented.**

When developing any type of technical training materials there are two primary considerations.

1. The specific information that must be communicated.
2. How that information is to be presented

Too often product training manuals try to present too much information at a level of detail that only serves to interfere with the learning process, also too often, product training materials present the appropriate facts but fail to explain concepts and the interrelationships between those concepts. The Sales Representative is left asking so what?

Effective Training Requires:-

Effective training requires it to be presented in short individual concepts to be clearly explained. The writing enhances rather than interferes with the learner's understanding. Is user friendly.

*   Essential information to be presented in short individual concepts.
*   Relationships between concepts to be clearly explained.
*   The writing itself is so clear that is enhances rather than interferes with the learner's understanding.
*   User friendly.

The instructional system must present the essential information needed by the Sales Representative to communicate with the health care professional in a clear concise manner that simplifies the learning process and contributes to superior learning retention. This approach provides a knowledge base that applies directly to "selling".

The training program must focus on the major issues facing the health care industry with learning programs on the rapidly changing healthcare environment and how to sell in that environment. Building long term customer relationships and the issue of generic versus brand name drugs. These programs need to provide critical background information required by the pharmaceutical representative to sell competitively in a challenging market place and should preferably be a 'self instructional learning system'.

Content of Information Should

Describe:-

* The Pharmaceutical industry
* A typical job description
* The Pharmaceutical market place
* Profile of a territory/customers
* Template of a product information sheet
* The managed healthcare system
* The hospital system/healthcare professionals, the formulary
* Physician profiling
* Healthcare professional audience

The advantage of using a self-paced learning system provides numerous benefits – saves money/time and is cost effective.

* Provides for pre-class training
* Lets the learner control the study 2-2½ hours at a time and provides self-testing in bite size pieces with answer feedback.
* Ensures that experienced and inexperienced pharmaceutical representatives come to the training room with a similar level of knowledge.
* Representatives test themselves to ensure a 90% competency or above has been achieved prior to head office training.
* Managers/trainer only need to review pre-class training instead of duplicating what is already known therefore allowing concentration on specific areas of need.
* New development of pharmaceutical selling skills program of similar design to learning modules allows an easy transition from "What do I know? to "How do I use what I now know?"

The advantage of using a self-paced learning system provides numerous benefits – saves money/time and is cost effective.

Representatives test themselves to ensure a 90% competency or above has been achieved prior to head office training.

E. Audience

Audience may be a mix of professionals and personalities

The new representative's audience may include physicians, nurses, physician assistants, administrators, laboratory technologists, pharmacists, and other healthcare professionals. Also, there may be several different personality types, including 'drivers', analytical types, 'expressives', and amiable people.

> **KEY POINT**
> Your audience may include a mix of physicians and other healthcare professionals with different needs, as well as a variety of personality types; you must recognize and address those needs.

Healthcare professionals have different needs

This section will describe how your sales team should target their audience for the most effective presentations, the types of personalities that they may find in their audiences, and how to deal with them.

Audience Mix. Different healthcare professional have different needs. For example, physicians will want to know prescribing information, clinical data, and the most current comparative studies performed with your product; administrators may want information on cost effectiveness, storage issues, and ordering procedures. It is important to understand the needs of your audience prior to making sales call. The information representatives deliver and the sales aids they use must be relevant to your audience.

Know your customer's personality type

Personality Types. They will meet several personality types when they begin their career in sales. Over the years, a model of the four styles of personality and behavior has been developed. Knowing the personality of their customer will help ensure a more effective presentation and increase their chance of establishing rapport.

Four basic personality styles

There are four basic personality styles: driver, expressive, analytical, and amiable. The driver tends to be very results oriented and works in the present. The analytical tends to be very facts and figures oriented and does not like to be hurried; analyticals often refer to the past. The expressive deals with the future and does not need a lot of detail. The amiable is probably the friendliest personality style and is influenced by people and relationships.

Driver. The driver has the following characteristics:

* makes quick decisions, gives orders, controls self and others, goal and task oriented.

* organized, logical, independent, and confident

* strong-willed, forceful, takes charge, competitive

* displays a sense of urgency, often impatient with self and others

* not interested in persuasion, does not rely on feelings or intuition, wants the facts.

* may be seen as critical, stubborn, and inflexible

* likes recognition for accomplishment of tasks rather than personal compliments

Driver is controlling, competitive, intuitive

Your representatives can successfully deal with the driver personality style by following the guidelines outlined below:

1. Reduce initial tension by giving recognition for their task efficiency.

2. Get to the main point quickly, use time efficiently, and be business like.

3. Ask 'what' questions to learn the customer's objectives, then find ways to support them.

4. Focus on results of the task, rather than on the personal relationship.

5. To voice an objection, disagree with the facts and logic of the situation, not the person.

6. Speak of goals, objectives, tasks, achievement, results, efficiency, savings, gain, and cost effectiveness.

7. Do not tell them what to do provide choices or alternatives; give them your estimate of the probability of each choice succeeding, as this indirectly assists in making a decision; the driver makes decisions quickly and is reluctant to change.

Deal with the Driver by focusing on tasks, efficiency, gains

Analytical. The analytical person has the following characteristics:

* problem-solving approach, seeks more information before making a statement.

* thoughtful, sometimes hesitant in a new situation or with new people.

* maintains a historical time frame: 'we'll do it the same as last time'.

* task-oriented, thorough, methodical, accurate, reliable.

* follows through and completes each task with precision.

* prefers a structured, organized environment with plans and guidelines.

* dislikes confusion, ambiguity, pressure, or persuasion.

* does not rely on intuition or feelings, works by facts and logic.

* may appear secretive or closed at times; may also appear critical of others.

* likes recognition for knowledge, problem-solving, precision, and perseverance given in a quiet manner, relating it to the task rather than themselves.

Analytical is thoughtful, accurate, structured

Your representatives can successfully deal with the analytical personality style by following these guidelines:

1. Reduce tension by giving recognition of their task precision.

2. Do not oversell or overstate themselves or their points; stick to facts and figures.

3. Do what you say you will do; reliability and dependability are very important – they will test you in this area.

4. Be organized and orderly in your communications; be persistent by adding proof and data to support your comments.

5. To overcome resistance to change and new ideas, be persistent by adding proof and data to support their comments; help this person avoid losing face with others.

Deal with the Analytical by focusing on facts, proof, details

6. Go over all details so there will be no future surprises.

7. Provide assurance that decisions and plans made today are the best ones and will not be changed suddenly in the future.

8. Avoid manipulative methods or gimmicks to force a quick decision, since this will weaken your credibility.

Expressive. The expressive personality has the following characteristics:

* interacts well with other people, open communicator, talkative.

* innovator, creative problem-solver.

* has a future time frame: 'It will be terrific when.'. .

* takes the initiative with people; motivates, stimulates and persuades.

* needs change and variety; impatient with routine tasks and excessive detail.

* may jump to conclusions by overlooking details and accuracy.

* enthusiasm may be mistaken for manipulation.

* seeks visible recognition for personal efforts, creative ideas, and ability to inspire others.

Expressive is creative, impatient, enthusiastic

Deal with the Expressive by focusing on ideas, solutions, agreement

Your representatives can successfully deal with the expressive personality style by following the guidelines outlined below.

1. Reduce initial tension by recognizing personal creativity.

2. Be friendly, open, enthusiastic and stimulating.

3. Present their ideas quickly and keep the discussion moving; encourage innovative ideas.

4. Ask "who, what, why and how" questions to elicit ideas and opinions about people, future objectives, possible solutions to mutual problems.

5. Avoid competing or arguing or win/lose discussions; look for common ground and agreement on action to be taken.

6. Take the initiative in handling task details and provide a summary of specifics.

7. Press for accountability since this individual may be more interested in the ideas than completing the job.

Amiable. Amiable personalities have the following characteristics:

* considerate of people's feelings, supportive.

* casual, friendly, approachable, people-oriented; avoids interpersonal conflict.

* has a current time frame: ' how do you think we should do it this time?'.

* understanding, cooperative, loyal, dependable, non-threatening, reliable.

* delegates initiative to others.

* seeks the support of others, particularly superiors.

* prefers discussions prior to making major decisions.

* may withhold unpleasant information from others to avoid hurt feelings.

* likes quiet recognition for personal efforts and people-skills.

Amiable is casual, cooperative, reliable

Your representatives can successfully deal with the amiable personality style by following the guidelines outlined below.

Deal with the Amiable by focusing on patience, feelings, assurance

1. Reduce initial tension by recognizing a personal contribution within a group; be sincere in complimenting.

2. Be cooperative, understanding, friendly, and warm.

3. Ask "how, why, who, what" questions and listen; show patience, learn about personal goals, and do not be pushy or domineering.

4. Clarify areas of doubt or hesitancy, avoiding overt pressure.

5. With disagreements, avoid a debate on facts and logic by focusing on personal feelings and opinions.

Session Objectives	Timing	Content	Method	Visual Aids	Handouts	Speakers
Morning Break	10.30 – 10.45					
Lunch Break	1.00 – 2.00					
Afternoon Break	3.30 – 3.45					

NEW REPRESENTATIVE INITIAL TRAINING

They should become familiar with these four basic personality types.

6. Indicate their personal support for mutual objectives; be clear about directions, actions, task assignments, time limits, expectations and follow-up meetings.

7. Interact in an informal, casual way.

8. Minimize risk with personal assurances and guarantees.

They should become familiar with these four basic personality types to help make their presentations run smoothly and effectively. Of course most individuals exhibit other characteristics as well, but one set of characteristics usually prevails.

Summary

Individuals exhibit other characteristics, but one set of characteristics prevails.

It is crucial for the 'new person' to be welcomed to the company the right and professional way. This should be in the form of a letter congratulating the new person on being selected from an exceptional group of applicants. This 'welcome' letter should refer to the fact that the manager, team and company are pleased to have the new hire join their 'District Sales Force'.

It is the industry's experience that new sales people who are appropriately inducted into a pharmaceutical company and know exactly what is expected of them, tend to adapt more quickly, perform more effectively and stay longer.

The audience your representative's address may be a mix of healthcare professionals, with various concerns to consider and different personality types to deal with. The four main personality styles are driver, expressive, analytical, and amiable. They should know the styles of their customers and the best way to interact with them.

Different healthcare professionals have different needs. For example, physicians will want to know prescribing information, clinical data, and the most current comparative studies performed with your product; administrators may want information on cost effectiveness, storage issues, and ordering procedures. It is important to understand the needs of their audience prior to making sales call. The information representatives deliver and the sales aids they use must be relevant to their audience.

Review Questions (Chapter X)

DIRECTIONS. Circle the letter corresponding to the correct answer for each question.

1. When developing technical training materials there are two primary considerations, (answer true or false against each letter).
   a. The specific information that must be communicated
   b. How that information is to be presented
   c. The amount of information that is to be given

2. The four main personality styles are?
   a. Expressive, compulsive, analytical, driver
   b. Driver, reticent, expressive, analytical
   c. Analytical, amiable, driver, expressive
   d. Compulsive, expressive, reticent, analytical

3. The expressive has the following characteristics:-
   a. Innovator, motivates, task oriented, stimulates
   b. Stimulates, future time frame, follows through, likes recognition
   c. Future time frame, innovator, motivates, stimulates
   d. Likes recognition for knowledge, stimulates, motivates

4. A Representative can deal with the analytical personality by:-
   a. Introducing change and new ideas, calculate risks
   b. Recognize their task precision, support presentation with proof and data
   c. Maintain a future time frame, change, exceptional results

5. Which is **not** one of the four basic personality styles you may encounter in your audience.
   a. Analytical
   b. Driver
   c. Compulsive
   d. Expressive

Answers to Review Questions

1.   A-True, B-True, C-False

2.   C

3.   C

4.   B

5.   C

II.   Class Training

This is the period of formal training that each new Sales Representative will have to complete prior to, being given a territory to work. The period of time spent in formal training will differ from company to company, however in this section we will present a generic overview of what topics your new Sales Representative will cover and be expected to have a working knowledge of. It is your responsibility as their District Sales Manager to mentally and physically prepare them for this formal induction.

The aim of formal class training is to provide Sales Representatives with fundamental knowledge and understanding of science and medicine to be able to perform their jobs with confidence and competence.

* Knowledge of the pharmaceutical industry and conversant on trends and issues that affect their healthcare professional customers.
* Knowledge and understanding of the role of pharmaceutical products in the treatment and prevention of disease, encompassing pharmacokinetics, pharmacoeconomics and managed healthcare.
* Pharmacology – basic principles of drug actions and interactions involving the therapeutical classes of medicines.
* We will use a product information sheet (PI) as the company document for providing the product information they will need to acquire.

The package insert (PI), or product monograph, provides very detailed and clinically relevant information about each pharmaceutical product. Clinical trials also provide important data on your product. Your salespeople should be intimately familiar with the PI and any relevant clinical trials when they enter a sales call.

Objectives

The following objectives are provided to identify expected learning outcomes. When you finish this section, you should be able to:-

1. List and describe the elements of a product insert.
2. Describe how clinical studies are presented to physicians in journal articles.
3. Compare the terms "features," "benefits," and "advantages" of a product.

A. Elements of the Product Insert

The product insert is the official labeling for any given drug. This labeling is developed by the company producing/promoting the drug and approved by the FDA. It is usually comprised of the following elements: the trademark or registered mark, generic name, description, clinical **pharmacology**, indications and usage, contraindications, warnings, precautions, adverse reactions, overdosage, dosage an administration, how supplied, clinical studies and references. The product inserts for all approved drugs are provided on an annual basis in the Physician's Desk Reference, known by its acronym, the PDR.

PDR contains PIs for all approved drugs

KEY POINT
The product insert includes the following sections: the trademark or registered mark, generic name, description, clinical pharmacology, indications and usage, contraindications, warnings, precautions, adverse reactions, overdosage, dosage and administration, how supplied, clinical studies and references.

Trademark and generic name

Product name. The product brand name is the trade name that a company chooses for a drug. These names are registered as trademarks of the company. The generic name is the chemical name for the drug. For instance Valium™ is a Roche trademark name for diazepam.

Active, inactive ingredients

Description. This section of the PI describes what the drug does and lists the chemical structure of the active ingredient. It also lists any inactive ingredients in the product.

Pharmacology: drug's effect, action, and metabolism

Clinical pharmacology. The clinical pharmacology of a drug describes interactions of the drug with the body. This section of the PI may be broken down into the pharmacodynamics of the drug (the effects of the drug on the body and its mechanism of action) or the pharmacokinetics of the drug (the extent and rate of absorption, the distribution, localization in tissues, metabolism, and elimination of the drug).

Indications and usage. The indications for a drug describe the approved conditions or disease states for which the drug should be use.

Uses of a drug other than those approved are considered "off-label." You should be prepared to deal with questions about off-label use of your products. Your company should have well-defined guidelines for dealing with the issue.

Approved indications and off-label use

Contraindications. Contraindications describe conditions or situations where using a particular drug would be undesirable. For instance, many pharmaceutical products should not be used in pregnant women. Therefore, the drug is contraindicated for use in pregnant women.

Contraindications

Warnings. Warnings caution the user/physician of possible dangers resulting form use of the drug. For instance, patients taking Valium™ should not operate dangerous machinery or motor vehicles until it is known that they do not become dizzy or drowsy from Valium™ therapy.

Warnings of possible dangerous conditions

Precautions. Precautions are measures that should be taken or that health-care professionals should be aware of before administering the drug. For instance, caution should be used when administering certain antibiotics to patients with impaired hepatic (liver) function.

Precautions

Adverse reactions. Adverse reactions are undesirable effects that occur when using a pharmaceutical product. These reactions may involve minor effects such as headache and nausea, or they may be very serious, such as cardiac arrhythmias (irregular heartbeat). You should be aware of and know how to deal with questions about the adverse reactions of your products.

Adverse reactions, side effects

Storage and handling. This section does not appear in all PIs. It is usually provided if the product requires special storage or handling conditions, such as refrigeration.

Storage, handling

Clinical studies/references. This section may include a brief discussion of relevant clinical studies for the product. It may also be a list of these clinical studies. This section usually appears at the end of the PI. Since clinical studies are an integral part of pharmaceutical sales training, it is imperative that you understand how these studies were set up, monitored, and evaluated. This information is discussed in the next section.

Clinical studies, relevant references

B. Clinical Studies

Pharmaceutical rep can filter large volume of information for physician

When dealing with pharmaceuticals, the demand for knowledge is high. Physicians are inundated with literature from hundreds of journals. This literature discusses **disease states,** products, and protocols. With this volume of available information on every product for every condition, how does a physician decide which drug is use for

---

KEY POINT

Journal articles describing clinical studies have several sections: the abstract, materials and methods, results, discussion, and conclusion.

---

which patient? This is where the pharmaceutical representative can help, by providing balanced information on promoted products. This demands a high level of knowledge from the representative on disease states, products, and competitors. By being well informed, the sales representative can present promoted products in a credible, informative and positive light. As a sales representative you will be integral in disseminating clinical evidence to support the use of your product.

Sales rep should recognize most important published studies

However, when more articles are published relevant to your product you must be able to recognize which studies are the most influential and which information within the study is most important. In general this becomes markedly easier once they have familiarized themselves with and worked in the field. They will start recognizing the 'principle investigators' that are most important in the field.

Elements of a journal article:
* **abstract or summary**
* **materials and methods (describes protocols)**

There are several different elements in a journal article, including the abstract, introduction, materials and methods, results and discussion/conclusion.

Abstract and Introduction. The abstract 'sums up' the findings of the studies. The introduction gives relevant background on the agent or field that is being studied and often cites previous clinical studies using the agent.

Materials and Methods. The materials and methods section includes information on the subject profiles, type of study, protocols used, and how the data was collected and analyzed. It is important to scrutinize this section when they are reading a journal article, for they may find that the study is not as 'definitive' as you originally suspected. For instance, imagine a clinical study supporting the use of drug A for condition #1.

The abstract has already quoted a statistic of 60% efficacy for this drug with this condition. However, when they look at the materials and methods section, they find that there were only 10 patients, in the study, and there were only 2 control patients. Of the control patients 1 of them healed spontaneously, therefore a 50% efficacy with no treatment. Do you think that this was a large enough patient population? For most clinical studies, these numbers would not warrant publication of the data. However, this example shows how important the materials and role in clinical trials. This section is intended as a brief overview of trial design and statistics.

Commonly used study designs are listed and described briefly below:

Several designs for research studies:
* open
* blind
* crossover
* parallel

* Open studies – both patient and physician know which drug (active or control) is being given.

* Single blind studies – patient is unaware and the physician is aware of the medication.

* Double blind studies – neither patient nor physician know if the patient is receiving active or control agent. The study is encoded in case something goes wrong and the treatment needs to be identified.

* Observer blind studies – one physician monitors the clinical response to a treatment while another adjusts the patient's medication but does not communicate this to the first physician.

* Crossover studies – patients take drugs A, then cross over to drug B and so on to compare different treatments.

* Parallel groups studies – patients on different medications are compared over similar time frames.

Statistics. Statistics for clinical trials are complex and often confusing. Three of the most important concepts for them to understand are **confidence limits, power** and **p values.**

Statistical concepts

Confidence limits represent reliability of results

Confidence limits, represent the reliability of results, given that two or more groups of patients have been lumped together and the average response of the groups has been compared. If there are many patients and the range of observations is narrow, the confidence limits are narrow. In this situation, a 59% response may be significantly different from a 60% response. However, if the range of observations is wide, the confidence limits will also be wide, making the results less useful.

Power is an estimation of probability of result

Power is an estimation of how likely you are to achieve the result that you expect. Before the study starts, a statistician will estimate how great the expected difference between two drugs will be and than calculate the number of patients needed to have a 80%.,90%, or 95% chance of confirming that difference. A 80% chance is not uncommon when a large difference is expected. But is the study compares two drugs that are similar, a 95% power may be required to show a difference.

P value is likelihood of chance result

The p value for a given result is an assessment of how likely the result is due to chance. A value of p<0.1 means that the likelihood of the result being due to chance alone is 1 in 10. Similarly, a p value of p<0.01 means that there is a 1 in 100 likelihood of being due to chance alone. In general p<0.05 is considered acceptable for clinical studies.

Results section presents outcome

Results. The results section catalogues what the outcome of the studies were. This section is the most data-rich section of the article and should be evaluated carefully. They may find it useful to generate a table summarizing results for quick reference.

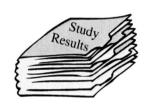

Discussion interprets results

Discussion. This section provides an opportunity for the investigators to interpret the results. Because most of the statements in this section are opinions rather than facts, this section tends to generate most of the discussion in the correspondence columns of the journals.

Conclusion

Conclusion. The conclusion is often woven into the discussion section. However, when separate, this section ties the results of the study into the current trends within the field.

C. Identifying Features and Benefits

Features and benefits can be viewed as the "bread and butter" of the product. Experienced pharmaceutical sales representatives are well aware that when they make a statement regarding their product, the physician, pharmacist, or other healthcare professional is saying to him/herself: "So what?" If they cannot identify the features and benefits of their products, their customer won't be able to, either! It is imperative that they are able to tie features directly to a benefit thereby satisfying the "so what" issue for the customer.

> **KEY POINT**
> **Features are attributes of a product. Benefits describe how the patient or the healthcare professional using the product will be helped by the product. Advantages are statements that indicate a favorable factor or circumstance suggesting superiority.**

Features and benefits should satisfy the customer

Features are product attributes

Features describe attributes of the product, e.g. a flexible, thin transdermal patch. Features detail characteristics of the product: flexible and thin in the case. Benefits describe how the patient OR the healthcare professional using the product will be helped by the product. So in the case of the flexible, thin transdermal patch (feature), the benefit for the patient would be a more comfortable patch. There is also a benefit for the healthcare professional – increased compliance in the patient, because if the patient is comfortable while being treated, he/she is more likely to be compliant. There may be several benefits for each feature. Make sure that they can identify and highlight the features and benefits of their product.

Benefits are helpful to patient or provider

They may also discuss advantages of their product. Advantages are those statements that indicate a favorable factor or circumstance suggesting superiority – an advantage states what the product does. They should be pointing out advantages of your product over the product that the customer is currently using at every opportunity during a sales call. However, they must back up their claims with clinical data if they are relying on comparisons to sell their products.

Advantages suggest product superiority

Why should a sales representative use features, benefits, and advantages?

To provide the healthcare professional with an opportunity to evaluate your product and what it offers compared to another product or service that they are currently using.

Sales rep can use features, benefits, advantages to compare products and meet individual customer needs

When should you use features, benefits, and advantages?

At every opportunity. However, we have to be aware of why the customer would buy your product and what benefits they as individuals require in order to make a decision. When the District Sales Manager is conducting 'the sales clinics'.

D. Presenting the Marketing Mix

Reasons for product preferences vary

Doctors differ in their reasoning for providing one medication over another – one physician might prefer an antibiotic supplied as soft gelatin liquid-filled capsules due to the fast rate of absorption. Another physician may prefer a liquid antibiotic that tastes pleasant because it is easier for children to take; there is less resistance and no painful needle. Still another physician may prefer using an injection because of the high initial blood levels of the drug, reliable absorption, quick effect, and compliance (the physician is assured that the patient received the medicine).

Sales rep must address customer's priority

> **KEY POINT**
> There are several issues that physicians are concerned about safety, performance, appearance, comfort, economy and durability. These issues make up the unique marketing mix that should be used for each customer.

Reasons for buying are SPACED

There are several issues that physicians are concerned about: safety, performance, appearance, comfort, economy, and durability. Each physician will have his/her own priorities for these issues. Your salespeople must learn how to come up with the appropriate marketing mix for their customers, supplying the information that they want to hear and highlighting the benefits that they deem most important. Talbot Smith, in his work on benefit selling, classified the reasons why people buy using the acronym "SPACED": Safety, Performance, Appearance, Comfort, Economy and Durability.

Safety. Safety is an issue that every physician is concerned about. Safety issues may include dose-related side effects, tolerance issues, and the potential for dependence.

Safety

Performance. Performance issues may involve speed of absorption, onset of action, tissue penetration, and efficacy of the product.

Performance

Appearance. The appearance of the product may also be important to the healthcare professional. Coloring may make the product more attractive for certain patients, or more 'fun to take' for children. Plastic containers have the advantage that they do not shatter, may be transparent, and are portable. Scored tablets may be advantageous because they may be broken to adjust dosage. Child-proof caps prevent accidents. Unit dosing packages allow for single tablet dosing, making therapy easy to remember. This type of packaging also acts as a deterrent to overdosage.

Appearance and packaging

Comfort. The "comfort" of the product may include how easy it is to digest, its taste, if it is chewable, and if there are any uncomfortable side effects. An older person with a throat ailment may have difficulty ingesting and
digesting medication. Soft capsules may be easier to take than large tablets. Medications that are pleasant tasting are more acceptable to children and adults alike. Chewability and the lack of side effects have obvious advantages. Keep in mind that comfort may be physically or mentally assessed.

Comfort for ease of use

Economy. The economy of a product may be described in terms of the cost vs. price or the value for the money ('economy size'). The difference between price and cost is this: price is what we pay for the product and cost is evaluated by what benefits we get for what we pay. Cost is generally measured over a period of time. Value for the money is what everyone wants. Price paid is relative to the effect. A large, economy size has a bigger price but lasts two and a half times longer.

Economy or value

Durability of effect of shelf-life

Durability. Durability may refer to how long the effect of a product lasts or minimum side effects over a long period of time. The lasting effect may result in only one tablet per day to control the symptoms. Long shelf-life provides a pharmacy benefit.

It is important that these elements are presented with the proper mix. The marketing mix typically has four elements: the product, place, promotion and price. It is important that these elements are incorporated into the original sales strategy for the products. Identifying each customers' needs will help ensure a proper marketing mix.

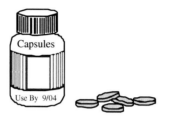

Summary

A sales representative must know his/her company's products thoroughly if they want to be successful in sales. The product insert and clinical trials are very important elements for providing valuable information to the healthcare professional. Healthcare professionals are inundated with clinical information and expect the sales representative to filter and distill important information from clinical trials to support the presentation of their product.

The product insert includes several different sections, each serving a specific purpose and providing specific information. Sections of the PI include the product name, description, clinical pharmacology, indications and usage, contraindications, warnings, precautions, adverse reactions, overdosage, dosage and administration, how supplied, clinical studies, and references. Product inserts are compiled for healthcare professionals in a resource known as the Physician's Desk Reference (PDR).

Clinical studies are valuable resources for the sales representative. Because healthcare professionals are accustomed to using journal articles as a source for prescribing methods, they will appreciate information about your products supplied in clinical trials. Most pharmaceutical companies rely on their marketing teams to provide the most definitive clinical trials to their sales force.

Clinical trials are usually supplied to the customer as journal articles. These articles contain several elements: the abstract, materials and methods, results, discussion, and conclusion. Sales representatives should know what information is provided in each of these areas and be able to use clinical trials to back up claims made during the sales call.

The types of study design used for clinical trials vary widely. Trials are designed according to the needs of the study. There are open, single blind, double blind, observer blind, crossover, and parallel group studies.

Statistics play an important role in understanding clinical trial data. Concepts such as confidence limits, power, and p values are important for recognizing the value of a clinical trial. Confidence limits represent the reliability of the results given that two or more groups of patients have been combined and the average response of the groups has been compared. Power is an estimation of how likely you are to achieve the result that you expected. P values give an assessment of how likely the result is due to chance.

The sales representative going into a sales call should know the features, benefits, and advantages of his/her products and be prepared to show how those features, benefits, and advantages can serve the needs of the customer. Features are attributes of the product. Benefits are the positive effects of the feature for the patient of the healthcare professional. Advantages are statements that indicate a favorable factor or circumstance suggesting superiority of a product. Representatives should point out advantages of their product over the product the customer is currently using at every opportunity during a sales call. However, they must be prepared to back up their claims with clinical data when making comparisons between their products and competitors' products.

It is important to get the appropriate marketing mix when they present products to customers. They must identify their needs and the appropriate product benefits for that customer. They can gain insight into what the appropriate benefits will be by examining issues that are important to healthcare professionals: safety, performance, appearance, comfort, economy and durability. The acronym SPACED will help them remember these important issues and understanding these issues will help them plan their own success.

Review Questions (Chapter X)

DIRECTIONS. Circle the letter corresponding to the correct answer for each question.

1. Which is **not** one of the commonly used clinical study designs?
   a. Open studies
   b. Single blind studies
   c. Random studies
   d. Double blind studies

2. Which of the following information is **not** included in the product insert?
   a. How supplied
   b. Inactive ingredients
   c. Recommended pricing
   d. Storage and handling

3. Clinical studies are published as articles in professional journals.
   a. True
   b. False, they are published in the Physicians' Desk Reference
   c. False, they are published in the Product Insert

4. The Materials and Methods section of a clinical study provides
   a. An overall introduction to the study
   b. Graphs and other statistics
   c. Information about the study subjects
   d. Summary of current trends in that disease

5. The term which describes how the patient or the healthcare provider will be helped by the product is called the
   a. Advantage
   b. Benefit
   c. Description
   d. Feature

Answers to Review Questions

1.   C

2.   C

3.   A

4.   C

5.   B

III. Post Class Training – Field Sales Training

This period of time is most critical to how well a Sales Representative will perform in the future. Prior to this period virtually everything in the training program has been theory this is now crunch time can do – will do? Sometime will probably have been spent accompanying an experienced company representative to 'get a feel' for what the job is all about by exposing him/her to a variety of calls made on health care professionals. It is now the District Sales Manager's responsibility to start the actual selling course on the new salesperson's territory. The following section will describe the method and process of 'professional pharmaceutical selling'.

Objectives

These learning objectives will help you focus your attention on learning outcomes. After completing this section you should be able to:

1. Describe the purpose of Field Sales Training.
2. Name the four elements of Field Sales Training.
3. Describe the role of a District Sales Manager when training new representatives in the field.

Key Concepts

1. Field training is critical to the success of the sales team and the individual.
2. The District Sales Manager's major role is in developing the sales force.

A. Training New and Experienced Sales Representatives

Training new and experienced Sales representatives is an ongoing process. Each person needs to receive appropriate field and conference training to bring them up to the standard of performance that has been set.

We need a training program to determine what their strengths and weaknesses are in knowledge and skills. Our major objective must be to develop in all Sales Representatives the level of knowledge, skill and communication needed to make a meaningful selling presentation on each of the company's major promoted products.

This objective will be achieved when the new Sales Representative is able to demonstrate to the District Sales Manager that during field training while using current promotional literature/reprints, he/she is able to:-

This objective will be achieved when the new Sales Representative is able to give a product presentation that is basically selling and not telling.

1. Give a product presentation that:
   a. Opens with a medical problem attention phrase designed to gain maximum attention.

   b. Follows a logical structure
   c. Coincides with current strategy
   d. Is accurate in detail
   e. Takes less than five minutes
   f. Is basically selling and not telling

2. Overcome the Health care professional's most common objections by:
   a. Recognizing the objection when it arises
   b. Clearly identifying the objection by selective questions
   c. Answering the objection with the assistance of third party reference (reprints).
   d. Asking for and obtaining physician's commitment to prescribe.
   e. Bridge competently and confidently to the subsequent product(s)

3. Demonstrate personal and professional integrity in business relationships.

4. Demonstrate the key competencies required of a professional

B. Field Sales Training – Manager Playing Representative

The District Sales Manager should plan to spend one – two weeks following the home office training working with the Sales Representative in his/her territory.

It is recommended practice that the District Sales Manager should carry out at least ten sales calls to physicians, specialists, pharmacists, other health care professionals to demonstrate how professional selling techniques are applied and to set the standard of professionalism that the new salesperson must meet and then exceed. Training new salespeople in the field involves four principles. Telling , showing, practicing, observing. The manager will apply these principles while he/she makes the calls.

Manager Selling (Representative Observing)

1. The manager discusses 'why' the call is being made, formulating specific call objectives and discusses with the new hire.
2. What it is hoped will be achieved, eg. Pharmacy call – the products to be sold, the order to be taken, (quantifying the objective).
3. What kind of opening? Statements or questions that will be used to identify customers needs, wants, concerns. Who, where, what, why, when, how! (Physician call).
4. What literature will be used? What parts will be highlighted, which reprints will support this, which benefits will be emphasized and in what order and how will they relate to the health care professional's needs.
5. What objections are anticipated – price, safety, performance, cost effectiveness, customer value added. How will they be dealt with.
6. What method will be used for closing or gaining commitment.
7. What bridging technique will be used for second and third product introduction.
8. What role the new representative will take during these calls and what he/she needs to observe.

The District Sales Manager should plan to spend one – two weeks following the home office training. Working with the Sales Representative in his/her territory.

Training new salespeople in the field involves four principles.

Tells

Shows

Practices

Observes

The manager will demonstrate how to utilize information sources by carrying out calls on the nearest pharmacy showing the techniques of how to obtain physician prescribing information.

During these training sessions the manager will demonstrate how to utilize information sources by carrying out calls on the nearest pharmacy showing the techniques of how to obtain physician prescribing information and how to sell and promote company products into and out of pharmacy.

The manager will also use fact finding techniques in the physician's office via the physician's nurse by using appropriate questions, conversationalising and creating rapport. When the District Sales Manager is satisfied that the new salesperson is 'ready to sell' and takeover he/she will revert to the role of coaching and counseling.

The purpose of this 'on the job training' is to provide the new salesperson with confidence and competence by demonstrating 'what a professional can achieve in the highly competitive pharmaceutical marketplace'.

The purpose of this 'on the job training' is to provide the new salesperson with confidence and competence by demonstrating 'what a professional can achieve in the highly competitive pharmaceutical marketplace'.

C. New Salesperson Making the Sales Calls

During this session of training the District Sales Manager reverts to the normal role being that of a coach. The manager will ensure that before each call is made an appropriate time is spent to carry out a pre-call plan with the following steps being taken.

1. Study of physician record card/history.
    If the information is not very helpful the manager will then counsel the rep on setting call objectives on what they want to achieve in the call despite the non helpful previous representatives notes.

    If the information is meaningful then the manager will assist the new person to formulate the call objectives based on the previous representatives comments.

The manager should use mainly open questions to have the representative think about and state.

(A)   What information is going to be discussed.

(B)   How it is to be presented.

(C)   Why calls are made – setting objectives

(D)   The kind of opening to be used – question or statement

(E)   The literature to be used, the highlighted parts to be fully discussed.

(F)   The benefits to be emphasized supported by facts and clinical reprints and related to the physicians needs.

(G)   The objections to be probed for and if forthcoming the technique to be used.

(H)   The types of closing that will be used involving trial closing methods and gaining commitment strategy.

(I)   The bridging questions and or strategies to be used during multi product discussions.

(J)   Post call analysis and physician records completion with the manager to determine from the representative:

* Were the objectives achieved and appropriate?

* Did the physician get involved?

* Were the questions the right ones did they provide the necessary answers? Were they capitalized on?

* If objections were raised –were they overcome to the physician's satisfaction?

* Was the call individualized or was it generalized?

* Were the right benefits used?

* Was the commitment to prescribe obtained.

As a result of completing the post call analysis, formulating a set of objectives based on information gained on this call for the next planed visit.

This format to be implemented on each call, with or without the manager being present.

The manager should use mainly open questions to have the representative think about and state information to be discussed.

Setting call objectives involving the presentation of products based on the physician's needs and wants.

As a result of completing the post call analysis, formulating a set of objectives based on information gained on this call for the next planned visit.

II. How do we Formulate an Effective Sales Training Program?

Effective sales training program should specifically define the following:-

A. Objective of training session

B. How you will evaluate the results of this training.

C. What will the standards of satisfactory achievement be?

D. Follow-up planned in field.

E. Required reports from Representatives.

F. The training methods to be used.

G. The training materials to be used.

1. Using contact report worksheets make an evaluation of the present skills of the Representatives.

2. Identify the areas of skill that need improvement for individuals and for the entire group of Representatives.

3. Select the most important training needs for individuals and the group – Rank 1 – 2 – 3.

4. Using the No. 1 ranked training need for the group; plan a training program to be conducted at the next scheduled Pre-Cycle Conference.   This would ideally cover one half day of this meeting.

    The plan should specifically define the following:
    a)   Objective of training session
    b)   How you will evaluate the results of this training.
    c)   What will the standards of satisfactory achievement be?
    d)   Follow-up planned in field.
    e)   Required reports from Representatives.
    f)   The training methods to be used.
    g)   The training materials to be used.

5. For each Representative, using the No. 1 or 2 ranked training need, plan a field training project to be used during field contacts with each Representative during the next three months

A.   Where Should the Training be Conducted?

1.   Conference room: During pre-cycle conference.

2.   Motel Room (when working in rural area).

3.   O.J. T. using proven formula –   Tell

Show and Observe

Practice

4.   Conference room – to improve selling skills, i.e. opening closing, bridging.

5.   Representative's own home – via cassette written questionnaire, assignment, computer etc.

When Should this Training Occur?

If you do not have an effective on-going Training Program in operation, you should plan to immediately introduce this in your next cycle conference.

B.   District Sales Managers Training Plans

The District Sales Managers' Sales Training Plans must be set in measurable terms in three main areas:

1.   The overall objective of the proposed sales training in terms of its contribution to the Company's total or specific marketing objectives.

2.   Its specific objective and the methods to be used.

3.   The individual objectives of training related to the job performance of each salesman.

C.   Training objectives in the three areas may be set out as below:

1.   <u>Overall Objectives</u> (i.e. release of a new product)

It is intended that as a result of training completed by April 14. The sales force will:

a)   Possess the new knowledge and skills necessary to sell the new product.

b)   Be able to use this knowledge and skill at general practitioner, managed care and hospital outlets.

c)   Be able to achieve the agreed standards of sales volume by district as set by the District Sales Manager.

If you do not have an effective on-going Training Program in operation, you should plan to immediately introduce this in your next cycle conference.

The District Sales Managers' Sales Training Plans must be set in measurable terms in three main areas:

1. The overall objective of the proposed sales training.

2. Its specific objective

3. The individual objectives of training.

2. <u>Method Objectives</u>

Training will be carried out by means of:

a) Formal presentation of plans by Sales and Marketing Management. The objective is to ensure that the sales force receive full information on the new product, full details of the launch program and is motivated to want to sell the new product.

b) Regional Sales Training Meetings: The objective of the meetings is to ensure that the sales force understands the information given, knows how to use it in selling the new product and demonstrates skill during role playing.

c) O.J.T. The objective of this is to ensure that the field force can demonstrate their ability on the job and are able to achieve the agreed standards of performance.

3. <u>Individual Objectives</u>

Specific additional training objectives for a salesman who has been identified as needing training in overcoming product objections i.e. product potency (norgestrel).

a) Know the company's six prescribed methods of answering potency objections (including authors, quotes, etc).

b) Be able to demonstrate his/her ability to use the six methods when selling the new product to GP/O and G/Family Planning outlets.

c) Be able to achieve the volume of business for the new product in each SRA of the territory.

Selling is a social skill which has to be acquired and essentially sales training should be aimed at improving the effectiveness of the salesperson's communications in face to face meetings with customers. The purpose of setting clear and specific sales training objectives is to ensure that those being trained know how to use the knowledge and skills they are taught and they are able to demonstrate effective use of the knowledge and skills and are able to achieve agreed standards of performance as a result.

O.J.T. The objective of this is to ensure that the field force can demonstrate their ability on the job and are able to achieve the agreed standards of performance.

Selling is a social skill which has to be acquired and essentially sales training should be aimed at improving the effectiveness of the salesperson's communications in face to face meetings with customers.

Example of a Representative Learning Contract Form

SELF DIRECTED LEARNING CONTRACT

NAME: ....   DATE: ....

Priority needs	Learning objectives	Learning Resources & Strategies	Date of Completion	Evidence of Accomplishment	Criteria and means of validating evidence

Representative's Signature: ....

District Sales Manager's Signature: ....

Summary

Health care professionals and their patients are becoming much more knowledgeable and demanding of the people who sell to them and the people who supply them.

In the introduction to this learning system we referred to the challenging times for the pharmaceutical industry involving the release of new products, increased pressure from competition and generic and therapeutic substitution, stringent government controls, managed care etc. We also stated that the volatile global marketplace demands more highly trained professionals than ever before.

Health care professionals and their patients are becoming much more knowledgeable and demanding of the people who sell to them and the people who supply them. We also referred to the fact that the District Sales Manager is responsible for making sure that each Sales Representative receives the appropriate field training to assist them in performing to the best of their ability.

The District Sales Manager is responsible for making sure that each Sales Representative receives the appropriate field training.

The District Sales Manager's objectives in working with a new salesperson should be to:

1. Reinforce the product learning knowledge that took place in pre-class and then initial class training.
2. Demonstrate to the new person how this product knowledge is utilized with the healthcare professionals on the reps territory.
3. Ensure that the salesperson develops good working habits in planning the territory, as a whole and then individual calls on the customers in the territory to ensure that the customer's with the most potential are identified and seen as frequently as practicable.
4. Develop a selling technique that is customer focused, communicates clinical practice guidelines, current disease management programs and demonstrates a good working knowledge of managed health care, and providing quality customer service with value-added.

Motivate and build self confidence within the new salespeople by demonstrating the professional methods of pharmaceutical selling.

5. Motivate and build self confidence within the new salespeople by demonstrating the professional methods of pharmaceutical selling eg. planning and organizing and administration required in a day in the life of a professional pharmaceutical representative.

Review Questions

DIRECTIONS. Circle the letter corresponding to the correct answer for each question.

1. Training new salespeople in the field involves the following elements.
    a. Telling, showing, criticizing, observing
    b. Showing, telling, practicing, observing
    c. Practicing, telling, showing, criticizing
    d. Observing, showing, criticizing, telling

2. Common objections to product prescribing are in the following list **except:-**
    a. Price
    b. Safety
    c. Bonus
    d. Cost effectiveness

3. The managers role is to help the new representative carry out the following **except:-**
    a. Develop a selling technique that is product focused
    b. Communicate clinical practice guidelines
    c. Discuss current disease management programs
    d. Is able to demonstrate a good working knowledge and understanding of managed health care

4. Open questions begin with the words, **except:-**
    a. Who
    b. What
    c. If
    d. When
    e. Where

Answers to Review Questions

1.　　B

2.　　C

3.　　A

4.　　C

XI. CONDUCTING EFFECTIVE SALES MEETINGS

I. INTRODUCTION

One school of management described 'meetings' as probably the major curse of the modern manager's life. Peter Drucker once said 'that spending more then 25% of his time in meetings is a sign of a Manager's Malorganization'. However there is another way to regard meetings. A large part of a District Sales Managers work is to supply and receive information and also to impart know-how. Well planned regular gatherings of the sales team, create the greatest opportunity for developing sales force performance.

These meetings also provide an opportunity to assist the decision making process an integral part of District Sales Management. However the quality and outcomes of these meetings have to justify the cost, so that means they have to be well planned, organized and conducted skillfully.

To be successful the manager must recognize the importance of the meeting and plan it accordingly.

Objectives

The following objectives are provided to identify expected learning outcomes. When you finish this section you should be able to:
1.   Describe the basic components in planning a sales meeting.
2.   Describe elements of knowledge that a representative must know.
3.   List the opportunities that a sales meeting provides.

Key Concepts

1.   To administer corporate training and development.
2.   Inform and get feedback from the sales team.
3.   Stimulate, enthuse and if necessary motivate the sales force.
4.   Provide a meeting place and forum for the salespeople.

Key Concepts

To administer corporate training and development.

Inform and get feedback from the sales team.

Stimulate, enthuse and if necessary motivate the sales force.

Provide a meeting place and forum for the salespeople.

A. Planning the Sales Meeting

1. Identify the purpose of the meeting. Which may be to:
   * Teach
   * Persuade
   * Communicate
   * Motivate
2. Set the objectives for the meeting.
3. Decide who will attend.
4. Establish the timing of the meeting.
5. Relate the timing of the meeting to the purpose.
6. Determine where training will appear in the meeting and what type will be delivered.
7. Check the location, etc.
8. Set the agenda.

District Sales Management involves a process of persuasion especially important when holding a sales meeting. It could be referred to as 'causing salespeople to accept what you want them to accept and like it'.

In selling to health care professionals your sales people believe that the prospective customers accept your product because they honestly believe it is the best one for their purpose. If the health industry customer does not believe this then it is the salesperson's job to convince them. In this sense persuasion dovetails with our view of pharmaceutical selling as problem solving: sales professionals who believe their proposed solution is ideal for a selected customer have a right to demonstrate this persuasively to the physician, pharmacist and other health care personnel.

A district sales meeting provides the manager with an opportunity to reinforce the need to each Sales Representative to re-examine the individual elements that contribute towards an exceptional level of knowledge – what specifically a representative should know.

Sales professionals who believe their proposed solution is ideal for a selected customer have a right to demonstrate this persuasively to the physician, pharmacist and other health care personnel.

A district sales meeting provides the manager with an opportunity to reinforce the need to each Sales Representative to re-examine the individual elements that contribute towards an exceptional level of knowledge.

B. Elements of Knowledge what Specifically the Representative should know

1. The Company
    Its history, objectives, organization, persons in key places, product range, sales volume, coverage and market penetration.

    (They must develop a sense of identification, loyalty and commitment to their company. This is only possible if they know it well).

    They must develop a sense of identification, loyalty and commitment to their company. This is only possible if they know it well.

2. Their Products
    The range, their indications, and their advantages and disadvantages in comparison with those of the competition.

    They must have a thorough knowledge of active ingredients, indications, contraindications, secondary effects, forms of presentation, packaging sizes, prices, results of clinical studies etc. Pharmacokinetics and pharmacoeconomics.

    Their products, pharmacokinetics and pharmacoeconomics

    If their knowledge of the products is not sufficiently comprehensive, they will be unable to promote them effectively to the doctors and convince them of their advantages or handle their objections.

3. Clinical Outcomes, Disease State Management Best Practice
    Representatives have to have sufficient knowledge to:-
    * be familiar with the illnesses for which the company's products are indicated.
    * understand the mode of action of the products.
    * master medical terminology sufficiently well to be able to communicate confidently and competently with their doctors.

    Clinical outcomes, disease state management best practice.

4. The Company's Polices
    Representatives must know thoroughly the principles and rules of the company which affect them and their work, their mission, their values and what the company stands for.

In order to be able to promote the company's products effectively, the representatives must know their doctors well.

To ensure good distribution the representative has to know.

Their clients

Representatives must know their territories like the back of their hand.

They must develop an itinerary and routing system to provide the maximum time in front of doctors, at the least cost to the company.

Their pharmaceutical markets

5.   Their Physicians
In order to be able to promote the company's products effectively, the representatives must know their doctors well; their specialization's, customs, prescribing habits, needs, methods, likes and dislikes, the size of the practice and patient profiles, the prescribing potential etc.

District Managers will have difficulty in informing each representative about every doctor on their territory. This is not their job. What they have to teach their representatives is how to investigate and use this information.

6.   Their Clients – Other Health Care Professionals
To ensure good distribution the representative has to know:
* which are the main pharmacies and hospitals in the territory
* what are their approximate patient volumes, which doctors are heavy prescribers
*   what sort of a patient customer mix do they have
* what sort of products do they recommend
* who are the owners and assistants, and what are their idiosyncracies/ special preferences
* what is the credit worthiness and reliability of all the accounts/ customers

7.   Their Territory
Representatives must know their territories like the back of their hand.

They must know where the doctors, pharmacies, wholesalers and hospitals are located.

They must know what days and what times are the best for making calls. They must develop an itinerary and routing system to provide the maximum time in front of doctors, at the least cost to the company.

8.   Their Pharmaceutical Markets
What is the volume and the rate of increase of the main therapeutic groups in which the company competes? What are the main competitors and 'factors that affect the marketplace'. Covered in the previous chapter.

*   The following pages are examples of sales meeting formats including product/cycle analysis, market position, strategy planners and product sales presentation format.

SALES MEETING PLANNING FORM

FACILITIES	CONFERENCE ROOM	PARTICIPANT REQUIREMENTS	AGENDA
Location Overnight Accommodation Eating Arrangements Charging/Invoicing Arrangements Message Handling	Flip charts Size Layout Chairs/Tables Lighting Electrical sockets Window blinds Water & glasses Microphone Overhead projector Computers Whiteboard	Note paper Binders Pens Name badges	Items requested Theme Finalized Circulated
		REFRESHMENTS	AUDIENCE
		Coffee break Lunch Coffee break	Selected Notified Briefed Visitors

SALES PROGRAM

SESSION OBJECTIVES	CONTENT	METHOD	VISUAL AIDS	HAND OUTS	TIMING	SPEAKER	CHAIR-PERSON
Example: to increase the level of knowledge specifically required to improve professionalism in selling.	Definition of knowledge Learning Principal knowledge	Lecture/Discussion	Overhead projector with prepared slides Power point slides	Session notes Copy of latest survey	90 minutes	Training manager	District Sales Manager
Example: improve objection handling skill	Resume of techniques practice	Video Role Playing	Computer screen	Notes on major techniques with examples	Video – 30 mins Discussion Role playing - 60 mins	District Sales Manager	

Program

Session Objectives

Content

Method

Visual Aids

Handouts

Timing

Speakers

Chairperson

LAST CYCLE ANALYSIS

Performance – Year to Date – Where you have exceeded or fallen behind your target for promotional products

LIST PRODUCTS	1. CALL RECORD		2. SALES RECORDED	
	CALLS SCHEDULED	CALLS COMPLETED	TARGET Mo./Yr. to Date	ACTUAL Mo./Yr. to Date
1.				
2.				

Last Cycle Analysis

Calls Scheduled

Calls Completed

Target Mo./Yr to Date

Actual Mo./Yr to Date

Last cycle analysis refers to the performance for the previous cycle covering calls scheduled v calls completed and sales performance target v actual month and year to date (two products).

RELATIVE MARKET POSITION

Relative Market Position

Preceding Survey

Most Recent Survey

Change

Source

Observations

MARKET SHARE Relative market share refers to			Personal Observations from Pharmacy and Wholesaler Interviews.	
Preceding Survey	Most Recent Survey	Change	SOURCE	OBSERVATIONS

the market share of your product(s) by most recent survey v preceding survey and change and includes personal observations from pharmacy and wholesale sources.

CYCLE MEETING AGENDA

TIME	TOPIC	DEMONSTRATION
		Overhead slides Powerpoint scheduled vs. Actual calls
		Actual sales vs. Target M.A.T.
		Specimens of competitive literature
		Samples or literature handout for clinical meetings.
		Copy of new clinical report.

Demonstration

Scheduled vs. Actual calls

Actual sales vs. Target

Specimens of competitive literature

Samples or literature handout for clinical meetings.

Copy of new clinical report.

District Sales Manager to complete the above cycle meeting agenda in preparation for a forthcoming meeting. Fill in the topics to meet the demonstration examples provided.

MEETING FORMAT PLANNER – (1 DAY MEETING)

Objectives for meeting

Last cycle analysis

Relative market position

Where are we now?

What must we make happen and how.

Pharmacokinetic review

Pharmaceconomic approach

TIME	TOPIC
8.00	1 A. Objectives for meeting B. Last cycle analysis C. Relative market position
10.00	Product (A) } Product (B) } Where are we now?
	COFFEE BREAK
10.15 12.30	2. What must we make happen and how. A. New visual aids B. Strategic approach
	LUNCH BREAK
1.30 3.00	3. Product update A. Pharmacokinetic review B. Pharmaceconomic approach workshop
	COFFEE BREAK
3.15 5.10 5.30	Workshop continues Practice selling to pharmacy, and physician selling using new sales strategy and sales aids. Meeting summary/action plan

SELLING STRATEGY PLANNER

PRODUCT		Select Appropriate Visual Material
ATTENTION: Phase Opening question/statement Main concept		Product visual aid monograph etc

BENEFITS	FEATURES	FACTS
1. Safety		Supportive evidence clinical reprints
2. Performance		
3. Appearance		
4. Comfort		
5. Economy		
6. Durability		

ACTION STATEMENT	

Benefits

Safety

Performance

Appearance

Comfort

Economy

Durability

District Sales Manager to complete this page using information from company promotional strategy.

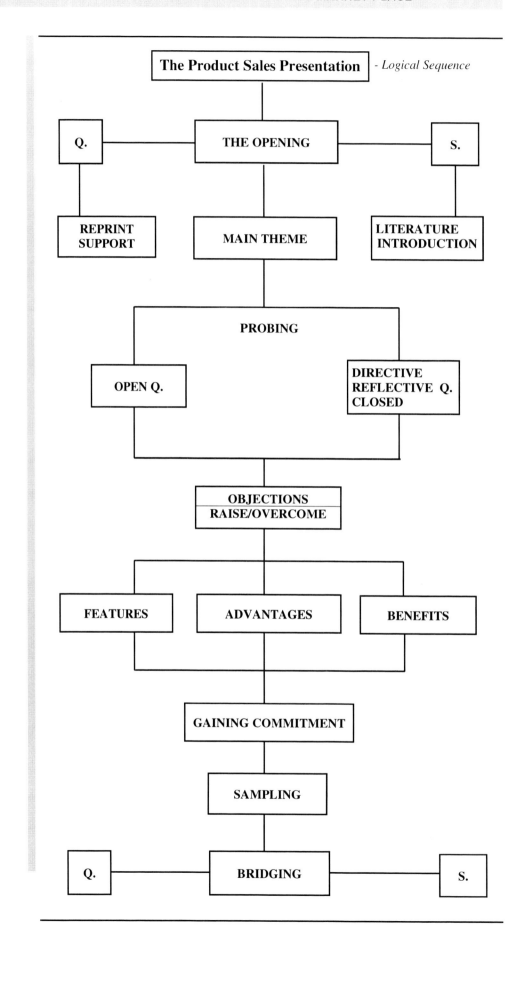

Summary

Sales meetings can easily fail and many unfortunately do. However, if the sales manager recognizes their importance, plans them carefully and runs them creatively and skillfully, they can provide an excellent training opportunity.

As well they act as a major motivational influence and an occasion when the manager can sell company policies and him/herself to the team. They key to success is participation, it is the salesperson's only regular opportunity to meet.

Remember a bad meeting will be remembered much longer than a good meeting, so make sure you have NO bad meetings.

Conclusion

Today's changeable marketplace demands more highly trained sales management and sales representatives than ever before. These are challenging times for the pharmaceutical industry.

Recently there has been a paradigm shift: where previously there was relative stability in the pharmaceutical industry, change is now the norm. Takeovers and mergers are commonplace. Historically, the pharmaceutical industry has been a product-focused industry; however, more emphasis is now being placed on disease states, treatment programs and customer services. An environment of cost effectiveness and therapeutic advantage has replaced the previous issues of efficacy and safety. The trend in hospitals is toward converting inpatients to outpatients of home-health recipients and emphasizing prevention rather than corrective medical treatment.

District Sales Managers are in a unique position to influence the success of their company by ensuring that their company Sales Representatives are exceptionally well trained, highly knowledgeable, posses the selling skills and attitude required to do the job they are paid for. To meet the expectations of Healthcare Professionals!

The professional pharmaceutical sales representative has to become more than just a technical expert, he/she has to become a problem-solver for the physician. More then ever before, sales representatives will need to earn the confidence of the customer through relationship building. Selling selectively and delivering a well-reasoned, compelling message are keys to success. Today's pharmaceutical representative must know the company, the industry, the products, and how to sell products effectively.

It is the District Sales Managers responsibility to see that this happens. Through the development of his/her management skills and knowledge. This learning system attempts to provide the District Sales Manager with the tools to carry out the major function.

Review Questions

DIRECTIONS. Circle the letter corresponding to the correct answer for each question.

1. Well planned regular gatherings of the sales team
    a. Allows the District Sales Manager to find out what the competition is doing.
    b. Create the greatest opportunity for developing sales force performance.
    c. Results in increased sales and profit for the company
    d. Inspires all team members to sell more competently and confidently.

2. According the rule of the six P's: Proper Planning Prevents:-
    a. Particularly Poor Presentation
    b. Plunging Profit Patterns
    c. Poor Product Positioning
    d. Poor Professional Performance

3. Factors that affect the pharmaceutical marketplace include all of the following, except:-
    a. Business goals of executives
    b. Changes in social attitudes
    c. Competitive products after the patent expires
    d. Government regulations

4. The life of a product has four phases: introduction, growth, maturity, and:-
    a. Decline
    b. Expiration
    c. Profit stability
    d. Revision

5. Developing a selling strategy serves to:-
    a. Meet company marketing objectives
    b. Promote advantages to both physician and health care professionals
    c. Save time
    d. Achieve all of the above goals

Answers to Review Questions

1.   B

2.   A

3.   A

4.   A

5.   D

THE BIOTECH BOOM

U.S. biotech firms total more than 1,300
New drug-discovery techniques are getting cheaper, faster, and better at targeting specific diseases. The end result is drugs that are more accurate, and markets will be more segmented.

360 DEGREE SELLING - HOW TO SELL BIOTECHNOLOGY PRODUCTS

prepares your sales reps to compete successfully in this new high tech, segmented market place.

Topics covered:

- ■ Scientific Selling
- ■ Consultative Selling
- ■ Relationship Selling

- ■ Managed Care / Institutional Selling
- ■ Territory Management...and more

To order, send check or money order for $24.95* plus $4.00 for shipping and handling to:
(Pennsylvania residents add 6% sales tax)

Black Dog Publishing Company
127 Longfields Way
Downingtown, PA 19335
Phone/Fax (610) 269-0479
e-mail: NewWavePh@aol.com
http://members.aol.com/blackdogpharma

*Credit Card Orders may be placed through Book Clearing House 1-800-431-1579 or any bookstore.

"The Biotech Boom involves selling completely new products to a completely new set of customers"

360 Degree Selling -
How To Sell Biotechnology Products
By
Vincent F. Peters

■ The only pharmaceutical selling book in the United States on Relationship Selling.

■ The biotech boom has created the need for sales reps to be more specialized in the selling of highly sophisticated products. The design and use of clinical studies in selling pharmaceutical products is thoroughly reviewed.

■ Drugs targeted for specific diseases require more skills in the area of disease management. Disease management is covered and tied into doctor prescribing styles.

■ Representatives are shown the principles of managed care and institutional selling and how the formulary systems of these organizations work.

■ Time and territory management along with routing and itineraries is covered. Many forms are provided to assist sales reps in more efficient territory planning.

■ "360 Degree Selling - How To Sell Biotechnology Products" is a necessity for today's pharmaceutical sales reps, no matter what types of products they are selling.

To order, send check or money order for $24.95* plus $4.00 for shipping and handling to:
(Pennsylvania residents add 6% sales tax)

Black Dog Publishing Company
127 Longfields Way
Downingtown, PA 19335
Phone/Fax (610) 269-0479
e-mail: NewWavePh@aol.com
http://members.aol.com/blackdogpharma

ISBN: 0-9656231-3-0

Approx. 86 pages, 40 illustrations and photographs table of contents, 8" x 11" trim size, perfect bound, paperback, $24.95. 35% discount to libraries, bookstores, distributors and wholesalers.

Pharmaceutical Selling Books Designed To Meet Today's Business Challenges

New Wave Pharmaceutical Selling

- The New Marketplace
- Pharmacoeconomics
- Disease Management
- Relationship Selling
- Planning and Targeting
- Recruiting and Training Sales Reps

How To Conduct Doctor Dinner Meetings

- Rationale For Dinner Meetings
- AMA/PhRMA/FDA Guidelines
- Pre-Meeting Management
- Conducting the Meeting
- Micromarketing
- Antihypertensive Case Study

Pharmaceutical Sales Management In A Changeable Marketplace

- Territory and Time Management
- Leadership
- Training New Representatives
- Coaching
- Motivation
- Communications

New Wave Pharmaceutical Selling $24.95

The book is about change in the marketplace and how pharmaceutical companies need to adapt to those changes. There is heavy emphasis on the two forces that are driving the pharmaceutical market place, pharmacoeconomics and disease management.
The rationale and principles of pharmacoeconomics and disease management are thoroughly explained. The disease management process life cycle and the four major principles of disease management are covered in depth. The New Wave selling process is explained, and spells out what pharmaceutical companies and salespeople need to do to be successful. It is an ideal book for anyone working in pharmaceutical sales, and is especially interesting for anyone who may be considering entering pharmaceutical sales.

How To Conduct Doctor Dinner Meetings $24.95

This book provides an excellent overview of the "How To" of conducting doctor dinner meetings. There is heavy emphasis on pre-meeting planning and preparation, and the AMA/PMA/FDA guidelines for doctor dinner meetings. The actual conducting of the meeting itself is covered extensively. Issues such as the role of the moderator, using the group, probing and listening skills, handling disruptions, and common meeting problems and participants, are all reviewed. Different types of meeting closing techniques and follow-up procedures and forms are included. The case study scenario for the book is on how to conduct a dinner meeting for an antihypertensive product. It is essentially a meeting planning guide.

Pharmaceutical Sales Management In A Changeable Marketplace $49.95

Managers are walked through all the skill areas required to be successful in pharmaceutical sales management. The book is designed for new district managers with less than two years experience, however it provides excellent information and tips for even the most seasoned district managers. The transition from representative to manager and the definition of management are completely covered. The management skills planning, organizing, leading and controlling are covered in depth. Each of the eleven chapters has its own set of learning objectives, review questions and answers. Checklists, forms and numerous exercises are included in the text. Good management practices and techniques are reviewed throughout the book. "Pharmaceutical Sales Management in a Changeable Marketplace" is a necessity for today's district managers. It provides the managers with the knowledge and skills required to be an effective coach.

To order, send check or money order, plus $4.00 for shipping and handling to:
(Pennsylvania residents add 6% sales tax)

Black Dog Publishing Company
127 Longfields Way
Downingtown, PA 19335
Phone/Fax (610) 269-0479
e-mail: NewWavePh@aol.com
http://members.aol.com/blackdogpharma

*Credit Card Orders may be placed through Book Clearing House 1-800-431-1579 or any bookstore.